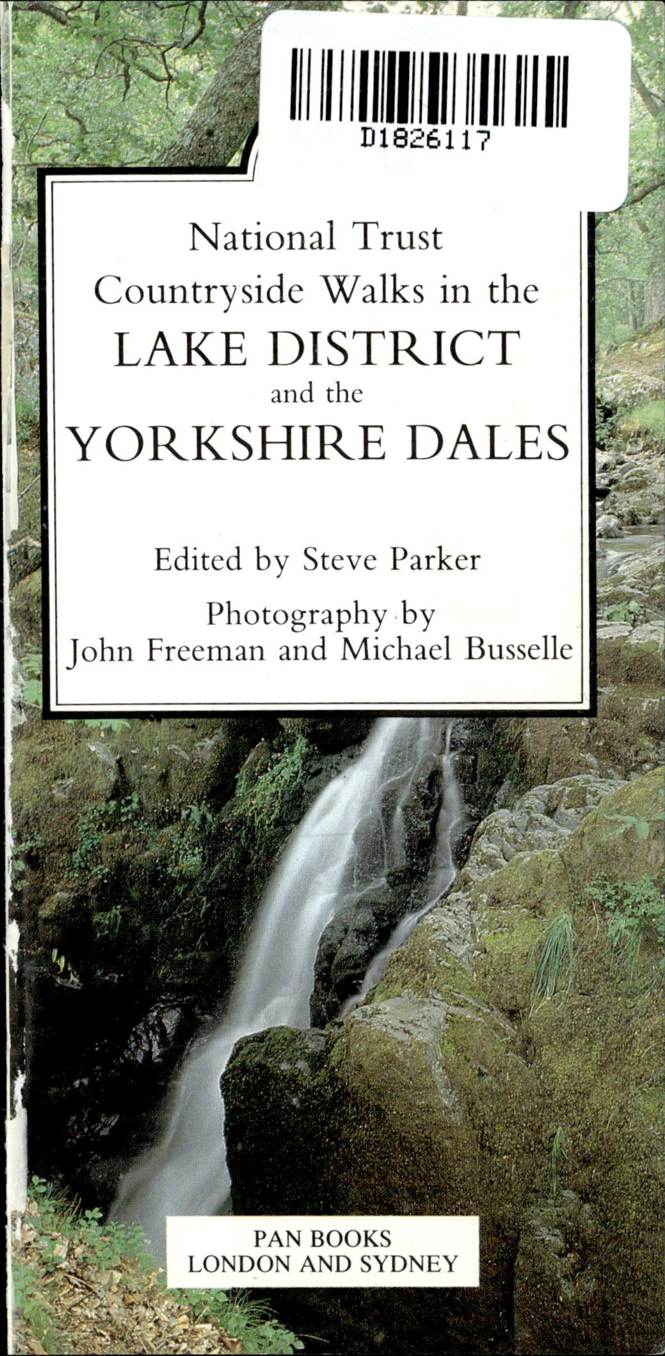

National Trust
Countryside Walks in the
LAKE DISTRICT
and the
YORKSHIRE DALES

Edited by Steve Parker

Photography by
John Freeman and Michael Busselle

PAN BOOKS
LONDON AND SYDNEY

Contents

First published 1985 by
Travellers Press,
59 Grosvenor Street
London W1X 9DA

This edition published 1988 by
Pan Books Limited,
Cavaye Place,
London SW10 9PG

9 8 7 6 5 4 3 2 1

© Hennerwood Publications 1985

ISBN 0 330 30390 2

Printed in Hong Kong

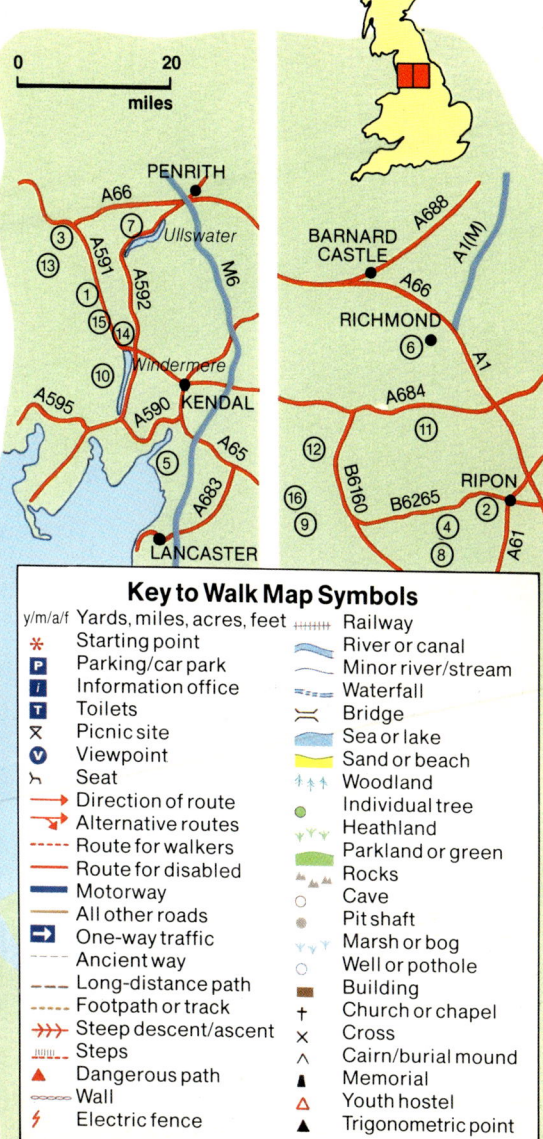

0
20
miles

PENRITH
A66
③
⑦ Ullswater
⑬ A591
① A592
⑮ M6
⑭
⑩ Windermere
A595
A590 KENDAL
A65
⑤
A683
LANCASTER

A688
BARNARD
CASTLE
A66
A1(M)
RICHMOND
⑥
A1
A684
⑪
⑫
B6160
RIPON
⑯ B6265 ②
⑨ A61
④
⑧

Key to Walk Map Symbols

y/m/a/f	Yards, miles, acres, feet	┼┼┼┼┼	Railway
✳	Starting point		River or canal
🅿	Parking/car park		Minor river/stream
ℹ	Information office		Waterfall
🅃	Toilets	⋊	Bridge
✗	Picnic site		Sea or lake
ⓥ	Viewpoint		Sand or beach
⊢	Seat		Woodland
→	Direction of route	●	Individual tree
↪	Alternative routes		Heathland
----	Route for walkers		Parkland or green
——	Route for disabled		Rocks
▬▬	Motorway	○	Cave
——	All other roads	●	Pit shaft
⇨	One-way traffic		Marsh or bog
– – –	Ancient way	○	Well or pothole
— —	Long-distance path	■	Building
⋯⋯	Footpath or track	✝	Church or chapel
⋙	Steep descent/ascent	✗	Cross
▤	Steps	∧	Cairn/burial mound
▲	Dangerous path	▲	Memorial
⌇⌇⌇	Wall	△	Youth hostel
⚡	Electric fence	▲	Trigonometric point

Walk Selector

		Length (miles)	Time (hours)
□ Easy □ Moderate ■ Difficult			
Number	Name		
1★	White Moss Common	$1\frac{3}{4}$	1
2★	Studley Royal	2	$1\frac{1}{2}$
3★	Friar's Crag	$2\frac{1}{2}$	$1\frac{1}{2}$
4★	Brimham Rocks	$2\frac{1}{2}$	$1\frac{1}{2}$
5	Arnside Knott	$3\frac{1}{2}$	2
6	Richmond & Hudswell	4	2
7	Gowbarrow Fell	$4\frac{1}{2}$	$2\frac{1}{2}$
8★	Brimham & Riva Hill	$4\frac{1}{2}$	$2\frac{1}{2}$
9	Malham & Janet's Foss	$5\frac{1}{2}$	3
10	Hawkshead	$5\frac{3}{4}$	3
11	East Witton	$6\frac{1}{2}$	$3\frac{1}{2}$
12	Upper Wharfedale	7	$3\frac{1}{2}$
13	Grange-in-Borrowdale	$7\frac{1}{2}$	5
14	Wansfell & Skelghyll	2 ⎫ 7 ⎬ $8\frac{1}{2}$ ⎭	1 ⎫ 4 ⎬ 5 ⎭
15★	Loughrigg Fell	$8\frac{1}{2}$	5
16	Malham Tarn	9	5

★ Facilities for disabled people. Fees payable at most car parks (NT parking free for NT members)

Start/finish P Car park	Grid ref	OS map 1:50,000	OS map 1:25,000
White Moss Common P	NY 348 065	90	Outdoor Leisure 7
Studley Royal P	SE 280 694	99	SE 26/36 27/37
Keswick Boat Landings P	NY 264 228	90	Outdoor Leisure 4
Brimham Rocks P	SE 208 645	99	SE 26/36
Arnside Knott P	SD 449 773	97	SD 37/47
The Green, Richmond	NZ 168 007	92	NZ 00/10
Aira Force P	NY 400 201	90	Outdoor Leisure 5
Brimham Rocks P	SE 208 645	99	SE 26/36
Malham P	SD 900 627	98	Outdoor Leisure 10
Hawkshead P	SD 352 982	90/97	Outdoor Leisure 7
East Witton P	SE 141 860	99	SE 08/18
Buckden P	SD 934 775	98	Outdoor Leisure 10
Grange P	NY 251 175	90	Outdoor Leisure 4
Waterhead P	NY 378 032	90	Outdoor Leisure 7
Ambleside P	NY 375 047	90	Outdoor Leisure 7
Malham P	SD 900 627	98	Outdoor Leisure 10

Introduction

Much of the land covered by the walks in this book belongs to The National Trust for Places of Historic Interest or Natural Beauty. The NT has twin aims: to provide access to its land and buildings where possible, but at the same time to conserve the landscape, its wildlife and its architecture. This means striking a balance between utilization and preservation. Walkers can play their part by following the country code, and of course by supporting the NT.

The rambles have been devised with novice walkers and family outings in mind. But being a novice does not imply being careless or thoughtless. You need to plan your day in advance. First read the walk account and become familiar with the route on good maps. Next, check ahead on opening times and work out a rough schedule of walking, visits, rest and refreshments. Equip yourself with the right kind of clothing

△ *A cairn on Loughrigg Fell, west of Ambleside, provides a welcome route marker in this lumpy 'mammiliated' terrain*
▷ *Miles of dry-stone walls cross the fells, with parent rocks behind*

and supplies. Out on the ramble, keep your wits about you: field boundaries may have been moved, trees taken away or new roads constructed.

To give you some idea of what to expect, the walks have been graded. EASY walks take around two hours and are generally well signposted along made-up paths and tracks. MODERATE walks take up to four hours or so; the terrain is mostly firm but there may be an occasional steep climb or rough track. DIFFICULT walks need careful planning, take the best part of a day, and demand detailed maps, compass, refreshments and suitable clothing.

In the Lake District, care in preparation is particularly important. On long walks habitations are few, shelter is sparse and the weather can about-turn in minutes. Yet walking in this wild landscape gives tremendous feelings of exhilaration. For the not-so-adventurous there are rambles with the focus on Lakeland wildlife or Dales rural architecture. Whatever your interests there is a walk for you – so put one foot in front of the other, and repeat as necessary!

Countryside Care

The countryside lives and breathes. It is home for many, provides a living for some, and plays a vital role in our economy. It is also the basis of our natural heritage.

Those who walk in the countryside tread a tightrope: between access and conservation, involvement and interference, utilization and preservation. The NT and other organizations are dedicated to preserve our heritage, by ensuring access to certain areas while at the same time planning for the future. Walkers enjoy the highlights of the countryside at their leisure, but they owe it to themselves and others to conserve these pleasures for the generations to come. We have rights, but we also have responsibilities.

RIGHTS OF WAY AND ACCESS

Public footpaths, tracks and bridleways are 'public property' in the same sense as a road or car park. They are not owned by the public; however the landowner, while retaining rights of ownership, 'dedicates' a path or road to public use so that a right of way is established.

A right of way means the public is permitted to cross land by the designated route, without straying from it or causing undue damage. If you leave the path you may be trespassing; if you leave litter, or damage fences or crops, you lay yourself open to legal action. A right of way remains as such until it is revoked ('extinguished') in law, by the local authority. It is irrelevant how often the route is used, or whether it is overgrown, or blocked by a locked gate or a heap of manure. In some cases, however, rights of way may be diverted to permit buildings, roadworks or farming.

Footpaths and other public rights of way are indicated on the Ordnance Survey 1:50,000 (Landranger) series. In addition, public access is customary in common land since fencing it to keep people out is both legally complex and impractical.

Subject to the requirements of farming, forestry, private tenants and the protection of nature, the public is usually given free access to the NT's coast and

FOLLOW THE COUNTRY CODE

The Country Code helps you gain pleasure from the countryside while contributing to its care. Here are some of its main points:

1. Guard against all risk of fire.
2. Fasten all gates.
3. Keep dogs under close control.
4. Keep to public footpaths across farmland.
5. Use gates and stiles to cross fences, hedges and walls.
6. Leave livestock, crops and machinery alone.
7. Take litter home.
8. Help to keep all water clean.
9. Protect wildlife, plants and trees.
10. Take special care on country roads.
11. Make no unnecessary noise.

Above all:

12. Enjoy the countryside and respect its life and work.

country properties at all times. Of course the country code should be observed in these areas as well as elsewhere. Much of the NT's land is farmed, so take extra care to keep on paths in these areas. Details of NT-owned land are given in *Properties of the National Trust* and local publications.

BEWARE OF THE BULL
Complicated bye-laws cover release of bulls into fields crossed by a right of way. It is best to assume that any bull is potentially dangerous and to take a detour or avoid it if possible.

What to Wear

For all but the shortest routes the walker should be properly clothed. Purpose-designed boots and a waterproof top are not only sensible for comfort and safety, they also help you enjoy to the full your day out.

The first essential is some type of water- and windproof outer garment such as an anorak, cagoule or coat, preferably with a hood. Modern lightweight anoraks can be rolled and stowed away when not in use. For warmth the main requirement is several layers of insulating material such as woollen sweaters. These can be taken off as the weather improves, or added to if the wind strengthens. Wool 'breathes' to minimize sweating yet retains body heat effectively. A thick, warm shirt is also recommended.

Denim jeans are a bad choice for legwear. They are usually too restrictive and have poor insulating qualities. Walking trousers should be warm and comfortably loose to allow movement without chafing. On long walks carry waterproof overtrousers.

Feet are the walker's best friends, so care for them. Strong leather walking boots with studded or non-slip soles are the ideal choice. Good ankle support is a must in rocky and difficult terrain. For short walks on easy ground a pair of tough, comfortable shoes may be adequate. Wellingtons may be suited to very wet ground but quickly become uncomfortable and tend to rub up blisters. Whatever the footwear, thick woollen socks (two pairs, if possible) are the sensible choice beneath. Footwear *must be broken in* and fit comfortably before you take to the paths.

On longer walks it is wise to carry a few extras in your rucksack: a sweater, a spare pair of socks, a warm hat and a pair of woollen gloves.

▷ *The well-dressed walker pauses to consult the map.*
Many people new to rambling are surprised at how chilled they become after a couple of hours in the open air, away from warm rooms or the car heater. Even on sunny days the wind and a few hundred feet of altitude can make you feel uncomfortably cool. The moral: Be prepared!

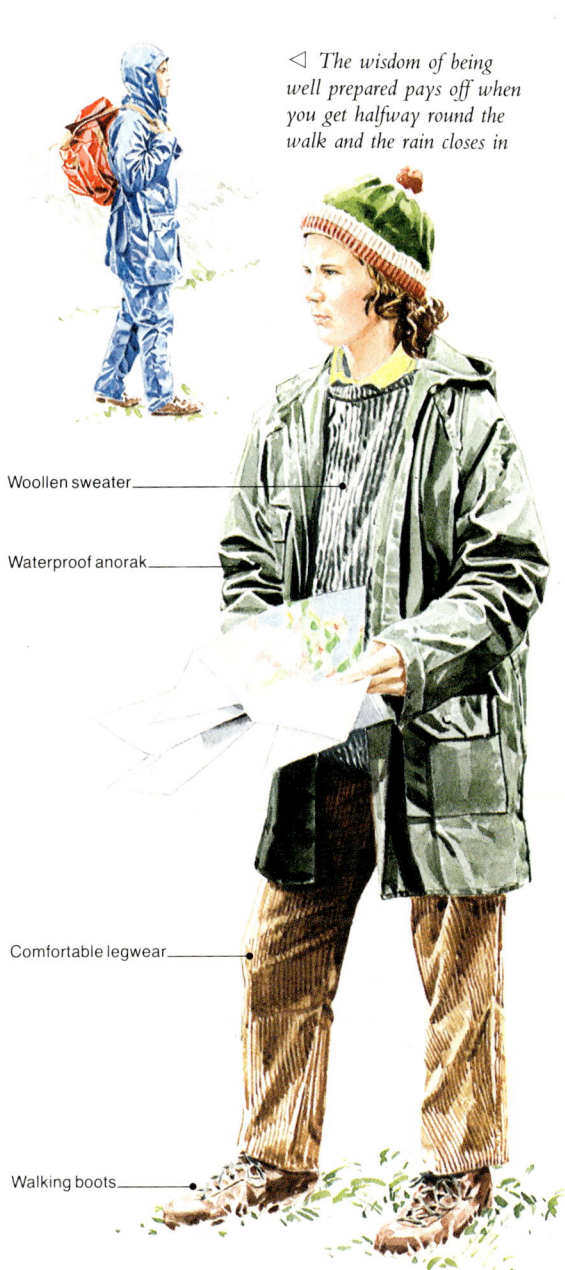

The wisdom of being well prepared pays off when you get halfway round the walk and the rain closes in

Woollen sweater

Waterproof anorak

Comfortable legwear

Walking boots

What to Take

Certain items are basic to any respectable walk. A rucksack and good maps are vital. Other equipment depends on the nature of the walk and personal interests.

The rucksack or backpack has many advantages over a hand-carried bag. With a rucksack you can take more, carry it more comfortably, and leave your hands free (an important safety consideration in rough terrain). There is an enormous variety of rucksacks available. For a half-day or day walk choose a medium-sized model of about 20 litres capacity, made of nylon or similar, that fits you snugly without chafing.

A selection of maps should always be at hand. Do not rely solely on the sketch maps in this book. These sketch maps are intended for use with Ordnance Survey maps (1:50,000 *Landranger* series or, better, the *Outdoor Leisure Maps* and others at 1:25,000, about $2\frac{1}{2}$

▷ *A hot drink brings a welcome feeling of inner comfort on a long walk, while glucose or chocolate bars provide ready energy*
▽ *Don't forget the nature-lover's second pair of eyes*

inches to the mile). A good map provides details of rights of way, viewpoints, parking, conveniences and telephones, and lets you identify distant features (see page 14). A compass is necessary for map-reading since paths are often indistinct or routes unmarked across open country. Local guidebooks and field guides point out items of interest as you go, rather than after you return.

On a long walk carry nourishment with you unless you are sure of a 'refuelling' stop. Concentrated high-energy food such as chocolate or mintcake revives flagging limbs and spirits, and a modern lightweight vacuum-flask provides a welcome hot beverage. A few sticking plasters, a penknife and a length of string may come in handy so keep them in a side pocket in your rucksack.

Walking is an excellent way of reaching an unusual viewpoint or approaching wary wildlife. A camera records the scene and 'collects' nature without damaging it, and binoculars permit close-ups of animals about their business. Walk with these items at the ready – you never know when they might be needed.

A compass is essential; a 35mm camera outfit is less so, though a pocket version may come in useful

Maps

A walker without a map is like a car without a steering wheel. It is essential to obtain good maps, learn how to read and interpret them, and check your route before you set off. Most experienced walkers use a combination of maps, as described below. The sketch maps in this book are not intended to be your sole guide: use them in combination with Ordnance Survey (OS) and other maps in guide books and local publications.

The OS maps come in two main scales. First is the *Landranger* 1:50,000 series (about $1\frac{1}{4}$ inches to the mile). These maps cover the entire country and show footpaths, bridleways, rights of way, farm buildings and other features. They are useful for general planning and for gaining an overall impression of the area.

The second main OS scale is 1:25,000 (roughly $2\frac{1}{2}$ inches to the mile). These maps are published as individual sheets of the *First* and *Second Series* covering the entire country, and as large fold-out *Outdoor Leisure Maps* for recreational areas, holiday regions and national parks. The 1:25,000 maps are often called the 'walker's maps' since they show features important to walkers and ramblers, such as field boundaries,

▽ *In the National Grid referencing system the first three numbers are the* Easting *(left to right), the second three numbers are the* Northing *(bottom to top), and the reference is accurate to within 100 metres (110 yards)*

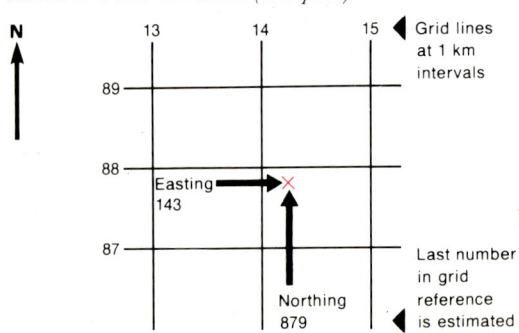

14

viewpoints, rescue posts and rights of way. Up-to-date 1:25,000 maps are recommended for use with the maps in this book. Further information is available from the Ordnance Survey (see address on page 127).

Another useful series is the *Footpath Maps* published by the Ramblers' Association (RA). These are at 1:25,000 scale and show many details such as footpaths, tracks, rides and bridleways, car parks and gates. For details of regions covered by these maps contact a local RA representative via a regional newspaper or community magazine, or enquire at the RA Head Office (for address see page 127).

Safety

Most of the routes described in this book can be completed safely by the average family, provided basic safety rules are observed. In more remote country, such as the Lake District, extra precautions are required.

1 Wear suitable clothing and footwear, as described in the previous pages.

2 Always assume the weather may suddenly turn nasty. Carry an extra sweater and an anorak, or cagoule, or even a small umbrella.

3 Obtain a good map and learn to read it. The maps in this book are intended for use in conjunction with detailed walkers' maps such as the Ordnance Survey 1:25,000 series.

4 On longer walks take some energy-giving food such as chocolate or glucose lozenges and a drink of some kind.

5 Allow plenty of time to complete your walk. A good average is two miles per hour, less if you enjoy views or watch nature at work.

6 If possible, have a first-aider in the group, and take change for emergency phone calls.

White Moss Common

A short, easy walk that incorporates a nature trail and gives visitors a taste of Lake District scenery. The Common is sandwiched between Grasmere Lake and Rydal Water and provides a stroll by the River Rothay, an ascent to fell land and views from Loughrigg Terrace, a favourite beauty spot.

The car park on the south side of the main road, near the River Rothay, is the start of this short walk (there is an alternative, Quarry Car Park, a short distance west on the other side of the road). The route is only $1\frac{3}{4}$m long but wanders through the delightfully diverse White Moss Common, one of Lord Lonsdale's Commons which are part-leased to the NT to manage as open spaces.

The path goes upstream along the Rothay River, meandering through pleasant open land popular as a picnic area. This used to be hard, dry waste from the quarry on the other side of the road until the NT spread topsoil, regrassed it and planted small groups of mixed hardwood trees. The path has been levelled and so is suitable for wheelchairs, which can be taken as far as the bridge.

Turn left on to the bridge and there are pleasant

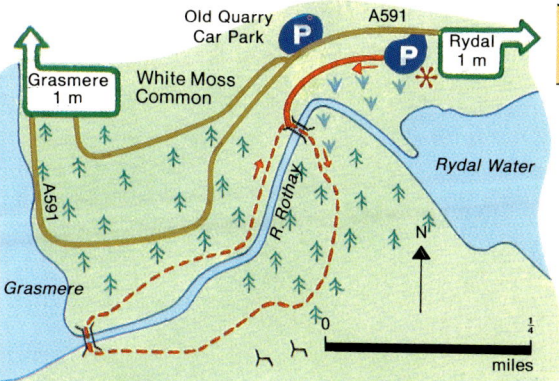

Old Quarry
Car Park
A591
Rydal
1 m

Grasmere
1 m
White Moss
Common

A591

R. Rothay

Rydal Water

N

Grasmere

0

½

miles

Car park: White Moss Common (NT) on S side of A591, 3m N of Ambleside. Grid ref: NY 348 065. Facilities for disabled.

views upstream and down. The Rothay looks deceptively limpid but runs cold and swift along shelving banks from Grasmere to Rydal, and bathing can be dangerous. Along the banks among willow and bog myrtle there is alder buckthorn, a species local to the Lake District. Wetland habitats near the water support a variety of waterfowl and this part of the Common is part of the British Trust for Ornithology's Rydal Water site, locally important for breeding, passage and wintering wildfowl.

The wood beyond the bridge is within the le

△ *Alder buckthorn is one of the brimstone butterfly caterpillar's food plants*

◁ *The River Rothay*

Fleming estate. Follow the path ahead, a right of way through land that has belonged to the family for centuries. Self-sown birches, ash, hazel and alder clothe the lower slopes of Loughrigg Fell and small bird life such as wrens, tits and chaffinches protest at being disturbed. The dry-stone wall to the left between wood and common is particularly well built; the cam (capping) stones are on a slant, and the exact placement of cam stones is often the mark of a particular builder. After a short climb, with a view of Rydal Water to the left, the path rejoins the Common through a gate in the wall. Press on upwards to the ridge and a splendid viewpoint at the end of Loughrigg Terrace (where this walk coincides with walk 15). Just above a welcoming seat it is possible to see Rydal Water to the right and Grasmere Lake on the left, both set in shining splendour among their surrounding fells.

The steep-sided valley that holds the twin lakes was gouged by glacier action; the receding glaciers left oval hummocks of boulder debris called drumlins. The island in Grasmere, mentioned by William Wordsworth and sketched, painted and photographed by thousands of people, is one of these rounded heaps of glacial waste. This area is full of association with the Lake Poets. Wordsworth moved to Allen Bank at the

◁ *Prepared stepwork on the rocky path through woods to the ridge and Loughrigg Terrace viewpoint*

▷ *Stone pillars support the upstream footbridge over the River Rothay, with the calm waters of Grasmere Lake beyond. Dorothy Wordsworth described the area as 'the Alps in miniature . . .'*

end of Grasmere in 1806, and Dorothy Wordsworth's journals are full of descriptions of walks in the neighbourhood. Hartley Coleridge, son of Samuel, lived at Nab Cottage on the far side of Rydal.

The route is now downhill, towards the upstream bridge over the Rothay at the foot of Grasmere Lake. Butterwort, an insect-eating plant with sticky lemon-coloured leaves and a small mauve flower, can be seen in the wetter patches together with lousewort. Watch the river for dippers, grey and pied wagtails and sandpipers. North, over the bridge and swinging right with the path, is Penny Rock Wood, managed as an access area by the National Park Authority. Sheep graze among the oak, beech and birch and leave little undergrowth, only enchanter's nightshade and wild raspberry.

Keep to the right as you walk downstream and leave the wood by a stile about 25y from the river bank. Now you are back on NT land, and passing through fields that have been grazed for centuries. Tall oaks line the riverbank and wildflowers star the grass. Biologists say there is a remarkably wide variety of spiders in this rich foliage. The stile at the far end of the field path brings you back to the bridge over the Rothay, and turn left for the car park.

Studley Royal

The beautiful landscaped water-gardens at Studley Royal and the magnificent ruins of Fountains Abbey, dating from the twelfth century, combine to make this walk easy on the feet and a feast for the eyes. Studley Royal Country Park also includes a deer park and the seventeenth-century Fountains Hall.

Car park: Studley Royal (NT) 2m W of Ripon on B6265 to Pateley Bridge; follow signs to Studley Roger and Fountains Abbey. Grid ref: SE 280 694. Facilities for disabled.

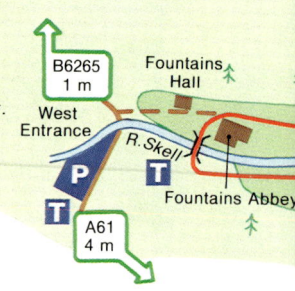

Studley Royal gardens were deliberately designed to be experienced from their eastern end, at Canal Gate. John Aislabie, former MP for Ripon, began construction of the country park in the first half of the eighteenth century. He and his son William spent vast amounts of time and money canalizing the River Skell and creating the formal water gardens. The 2m walk allows the majestic climax of Fountains Abbey ruins to be seen and appreciated from a distance.

Drive to the estate from Studley Roger, through the triumphal arch main gate and past the deer grazing in their parkland. From the car park beside the lake pass through the Canal Gate and turn left behind the shop and restaurant (formerly a lodge, built in 1850). Cross the River Skell above the weir, by the wooden bridge or the modern stepping stones. This stretch of the River Skell is called the Canal, hence the Canal Gate. The two Fishing Tabernacles and Rusticated Piers date

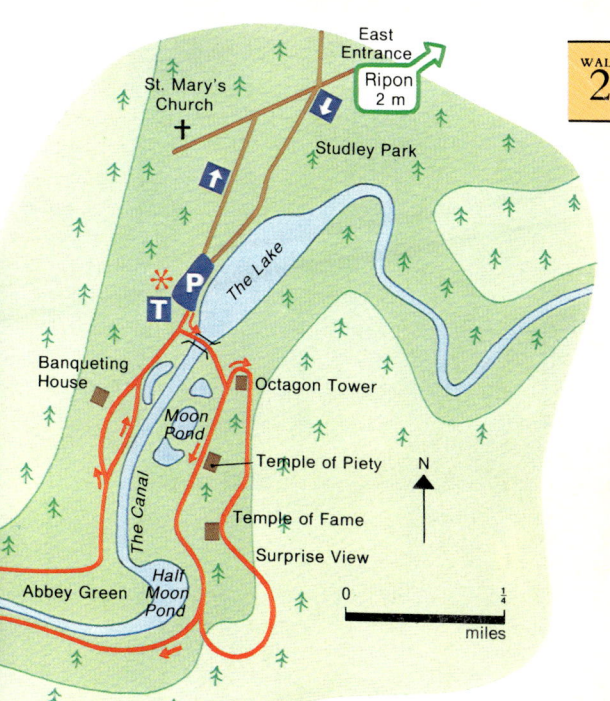

East
Entrance
Ripon
2 m

St. Mary's
Church

Studley Park

The Lake

P

T

*

Banqueting
House

Octagon Tower

Moon
Pond

Temple of Piety

The Canal

Temple of Fame

Surprise View

N

Abbey Green

Half
Moon
Pond

0   ¼

miles

from 1728. Turn right and the path leads at an angle away from the river to the Oval Moon Pond, overlooked by the Temple of Piety (1740–42). This Roman Doric structure was designed as a cool summer-house on the more shady side of the valley.

The level path continues westwards below the woodland to the Half Moon Pond. If you keep to the outer (left-hand) side of the pond you will soon be rewarded by a view of Fountains Abbey nearly ½m away. However, it is more worthwhile to take the upper path, by retracing your steps 100y from the Temple of Piety and following a path that climbs steeply through the woods. You enter a 50y curving tunnel cut through limestone and emerge into a pleasant glade overlooked by the Octagon Tower. Built in 1728, its view is now largely obscured by trees.

Walk away from the tower, keeping the valley on your right. After 200y the good woodland track

△ *The canalized River Skell flows slowly through Studley Royal Park*

reaches the Temple of Fame, moved to this site from across the valley in 1781 to mark William's (John Aislabie's son) 60th year as MP for Ripon. Continue to the Surprise View, where an opening in the wooden shelter allows a superb vista up the valley to Fountains Abbey. From the shelter a path curves down to the main track by Half Moon Pond, and it is then a straightforward walk along the waterside to the abbey ruins.

Detailed guide books tell the full story of Fountains Abbey, and tours of the ruins are regularly provided. Suffice to say here that, after its foundation in 1132, the abbey was occupied and used by Cistercian monks until the Dissolution in 1539. The extensive ruins represent growth and development over four centuries, followed by gradual decay; they are probably Europe's finest Cistercian monastic ruins and are worth a thorough exploration.

Return along the north side of the valley and on the right at the eastern end of Abbey Green, before the path enters woodland, you will see the low remains of the precinct wall running down to the river. This wall, originally up to ten feet high, represented the eastern boundary of the abbey land. The path swings to the left and climbs slightly; at the fork keep left and, still

▷ *Ragged robin is fairly
common in damp places, and
at Studley several of the
shadier cracks in the
stonework of the temples are
home to this perennial. From
May to July its blooms
attract bees and butterflies*

◁ *Common birdsfoot-trefoil
grows in the drier areas at
Studley. It has dozens of
local names, including
'Bacon-and-eggs'*

climbing, you reach the Banqueting House (1728–38). This was used during the summer for small party functions away from the mansion. The original view across the Canal to the Temple of Piety, Temple of Fame and Octagon Tower is now partly obscured. Follow the path a short distance to the east and the East Gate and car park are only a few yards away.

Throughout the walk there is an abundance of wildlife in the rich diversity of habitats – woodland, grassland, water, and rocks or stones. Perhaps the Canada geese, mallard, coot and moorhens are most prominent on the open water. Botanists will delight in the ground flora of the woods and open grassland, while everyone can appreciate the variety of native and introduced trees.

As an epilogue to the walk consider a visit to St Mary's Church above the car park. William Burges' High-Gothic Victorian design (1871–78) is magnificent, and a landscaped avenue extends 3m eastwards from the church to Ripon Cathedral to provide a memorable visual climax.

△ *The Temple of Piety gazes across the calm waters of the Oval Moon Pond*
◁ *Lilies and rushes thrive in the slow-moving Skell waters and still ponds on the estate*

▽ *Fountains Abbey became part of the Studley property in 1768; in 1983 the NT acquired the entire estate. The Abbey predates its landscaping by six centuries*

Friar's Crag

This beautiful shore walk skirts the Friar's
Crag promontory jutting into Derwent
Water. The open views of the lake to the
south from the oak and beech woods contrast
with the towering backdrop of Skiddaw and
Londscale Fell to the north.

An easy and relatively flat walk of 2½m, this ramble still
reveals excellent Lake District scenery. The route is
entirely on NT land and visits Friar's Crag, a lakeside
mass of igneous rock thrust in molten state into the
indigenous Skiddaw slate.

Turn left out of the public car park, with the 40a
Crow Park on the right. The road ends at the Boat
Landings, which provide boat hire and a launch service
round Derwent Water. The NT Information Centre
opposite the boats stocks a leaflet on the walk and the
nature trail, and information for wheelchair visitors.

The path follows the lake shore with a clear view of
Derwent Island, NT-owned but open to the public
only by invitation. In Elizabethan times the Company
of Mines Royal had a brewery there and a garden; at
the end of the eighteenth century a Gothic house was
built for a Mr Pocklington, also a battery for cannon, a
chapel and a Druid's circle which was washed away in
a storm. On the left are the old stables for Derwent
Island and two cottages let to NT tenants.

Across the water is Brandelhow Woods nestling
under Cat Bells, the first Lake District property
acquired by the NT through the efforts of Canon
Rawnsley, Vicar of Crosthwaite near Keswick. On his
death in 1920 Friar's Crag, together with Lord's Island
and Calf Close Bay, were given to the NT as his
memorial and a plaque is set in the wall beside the path.

As you approach the Crag itself, pause to admire the
memorial to the poet John Ruskin – a slab of natural
rock with a bronze portrait medallion. A few yards
further a crown of Scots pine on the Crag signals the
famous view. Its composition of hill and water is very
nearly perfect, leading the eye to the southern end of

KESWICK

KESWICK

B5289

P

*

Crow Park

Cockshot
Wood

Castle
Head

i

T

Boat
Landings

Rawnsley Memorial

Brockle Beck

Saw Mill

Ruskin Memorial

Derwent
Isle

N

Friar's
Crag

The
Ings

0   ¼

miles

Stable Hills

Lord's
Island

Derwent Water

Broom Point

P

Great
Wood

Calf Close Bay

Borrowdale
5 m

Car park: Keswick Boat
Landings, NE shore of
Derwent Water ¼m S of
Keswick. Leave town on
B5289 (to Borrowdale),
turn right at roundabout
signposted *To the Lake*.
Grid ref: NY 264 228.   Facilities for disabled.

△ *Small craft drawn up on Derwent Water's shingle shore*

Close examination of muddy and soft ground, as in Great Wood on the Friar's Crag walk, may reveal footprints of other 'walkers'. Look particularly at stream and pond edges, where animals come to drink

△ *Common fox*

◁ *Weasel*

Mink ▷

◁ *Badger*

△ *Derwent Water from the shore path. The NT owns much of the surrounding land, including 562a of the lake itself, more specifically the bed of its western half*
◁ *One of John Ruskin's first memories was 'the intense joy, mingled with awe' at the view of Derwent Water*

the lake and Castle Crag, a small conical hill known as 'the Tooth of Borrowdale'. To your left is Lord's Island, once a seat of the Earls of Derwent Water, and the island beyond to the right is St Herbert's Isle, where the saint is said to have lived. Rampsholme is the smaller island in the middle, a favourite roosting place for cormorants. All three islands are protected by the NT.

From the Crag the path goes along the lakeshore, while wheelchairs return a few yards on the original path to take a levelled route to the right through a widened gate. From this point the circular route for wheelchairs is advised only for those who have strong helpers.

Beyond the open fields bordered by fine old oak is Ings Wood. The land to the left of the path is swampy and colonized by alder, willow and marsh plants. Cross the bridge over Brockle Beck to an open area of grass and a view of Walla Crag, and the wood ends at a wicket gate. Note the track to the left which crosses your path and leads to the buildings of Stable Hills on the right. From here to the next view at Broom Point the path is still negotiable for wheelchairs but these should return from the Point to the wicket gate and take the track to the left, to avoid rough ground

△ *The shady lakeshore woods are alive with birds in summer, when you may hear the machine-gun bursts of the great spotted woodpecker*
▷ *Looking south-west across Derwent Water to the Derwent Fells beyond*

through Great Wood.

Walk on to Broom Point, where the views are similar to those from Friar's Crag. Turner sketched in these fields and you may see cormorant, mallard, coot, tufted duck and golden-eye bobbing and diving on the lake. The path curves left and right round Calf Close Bay, then near a large patch of wild yellow iris it turns left off the shingle beach into Great Wood and runs north parallel to the Borrowdale road. The wall that divides the wood from the road is built of water-smoothed boulders from the lake. Across the road the rest of Great Wood rises up the fell, concealing a large NT car park.

The path runs through groves of mature oak and beech which are nearing the end of their natural lives; the NT are planting replacements – including Spanish chestnuts and cedars of Lebanon – to maintain the woodland mosaic. In wet weather examine muddy areas for tracks of fox, badger, weasel and mink. There is a particularly magnificent horse chestnut at the point where the path crosses the Stable Hills farm track and

wheelchairs rejoin the route from the left.

Out of the wood the early eighteenth-century Boow Barn comes into view on the other side of the road; this is now used as a sawmill. Beyond is Castle Head, a conical hill 529f high, cloaked with ancient oaks and topped by bare rock. This is the core of an extinct volcano and from the top is one of the finest views in the valley. If you wish, go through the convenient hedge-gap and climb to the summit as a detour to the route.

Opposite Castle Head, just before a small rise, turn left down steps – with a ramp for wheelchairs – to cross a field towards Cockshot Wood. There are views across the meadows to rugged Walla Crag and the Grange Fells before the path plunges into the trees. Wheelchairs should take the left-hand path and then first right to the Boat Landings, while walkers follow the track straight ahead over a small rise. Finches, yellowhammers and wrens dwell in the wood and the great spotted woodpecker is a constant visitor. Top the rise and you are back at the Landings.

Brimham Rocks

Brimham Rocks, near Ripon, are in fine walking country and this short route is an alternative to the longer walk 8. The ramble takes in heath, field, wood and farmland and also visits Brimham House NT Information Centre.

This walk has been selected to provide an easy yet interesting $2\frac{1}{2}$m route that visits the weirdly-shaped Brimham Rocks and the Brimham House NT Information Centre, where there is an audio–visual display explaining how the rocks were formed.

From the car park near the southern end of the Brimham property, follow the main access track north to Brimham House. Many short side paths give detours to the fascinating formations and much time can be spent exploring and enjoying these. An all-weather path suitable for wheelchairs short-cuts the main route, passing close to the Castle Rocks group of large tors, and rejoins the main path below Brimham House.

△ *The eroded millstone grit formations at Brimham*
▷ *Vegetation has regrown since NT acquisition in 1970*

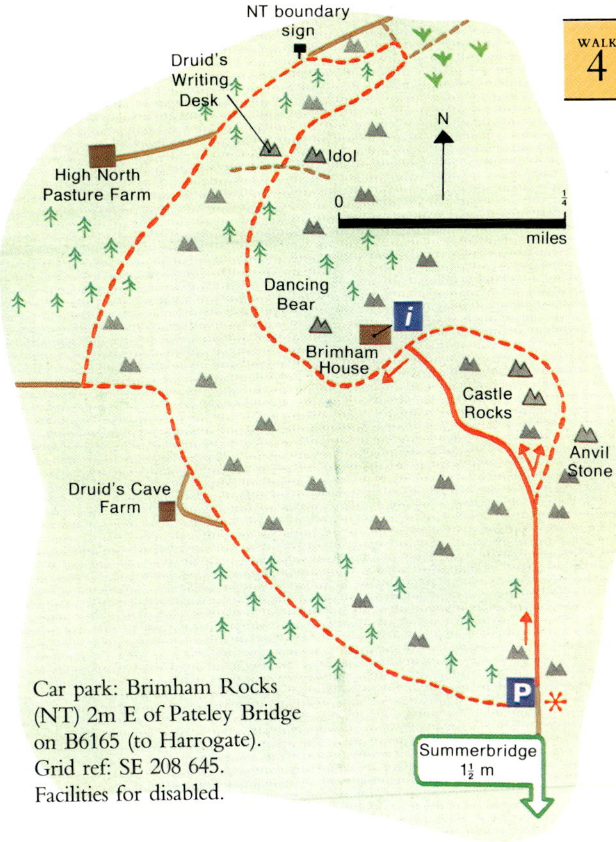

NT boundary
sign

Druid's
Writing
Desk

Idol

High North
Pasture Farm

N

Druid's
Writing
Desk

0 _____ ¼
miles

Dancing
Bear

i

Brimham
House

Castle
Rocks

Anvil
Stone

Druid's Cave
Farm

Car park: Brimham Rocks
(NT) 2m E of Pateley Bridge
on B6165 (to Harrogate).
Grid ref: SE 208 645.
Facilities for disabled.

P
✳

Summerbridge
1½ m

33

Continue along the path to the left (west) of Brimham House, soon passing the Dancing Bear Rock on the right. At the first junction of paths keep straight past the mushroom-shaped Druid's Writing-Desk Rock to the left and the Idol Rock to the right. Beyond the last of the rock formations the path, now narrower, swings right towards open heather moor. After a few yards fork left and then left again on to a narrow, sandy path that descends gently through a narrow space between banks; in 50y fork left again, with young birches on your left. For a while the track becomes grassier, and after passing more rocks on the right you descend to join a white, stony lane by a *NT Boundary* sign.

Turn left and follow the lane, through birches, towards North Pasture Farm. Where the farm track turns right to the farm buildings you keep straight and go through two gates. After the second, bear slightly

◁ *The striking red berries of rowan (mountain ash) glow on a small specimen clinging to a crevice in the sandstone rock*

△ *Damp moor surrounds much of the lower Brimham site*
▽ *Close-up of the eroded surfaces; one ancient legend says Druids fashioned the wonderful shapes*

Many fine rowans (mountain ash) grow in the Dales; their red berries are a feast for birds

right away from the stone wall on your left. Cross pasture to another gate 200y away, descend a slight slope for a similar distance with a wall to your left, and aim for the corner of the field by a wood where a stone stile takes the path into the trees. Walk through the wood for 150y to its southern edge, and look for a stone stile by a holly tree. Traverse the stile into rough pasture and cross this directly for 200y to join a farm track. Turn left on this, up the hill to a blue iron gate which incorporates a stile. Beyond this a walled lane leads ahead, through a gate, with a wall to the right and beyond, and rough ground to the left. Follow the obvious stony, whitish farm track, passing Druid's Cave Farm (NT) on the right, into birch and rowan woodland. In about $\frac{1}{3}$m this lane brings you to the southern entrance of Brimham Rocks and back to the car park.

△ *Vegetation clings to the undercut rock strata*

▽ *A view over the rocks to Brimham House*

Barns in the Dales

Some of the most characteristic buildings in the Yorkshire Dales are the detached stone barns dotted about in the valleys and on the hillsides. In the traditional Dales system of pastoral farming, probably unique in Britain, barns were built where they were most needed – out in the fields, away from the farmhouse. The barn stored hay from surrounding fields, and the hay was used to fodder cattle also housed in the barn from the end of November to early May.

In Swaledale and the northern dales a barn is sometimes called a cowhouse or fieldhouse; south of Wensleydale, and particularly in Wharfedale and the Craven area, it is usually referred to as a laithe. Over most of the Dales the part occupied by cows is known as the shippon, or the mistal in Nidderdale and lower Wharfedale. Hay is stored in the hay-mow; in Swaledale barns this extends from ground to rafters, sometimes with an additional loft above the cattle-standings (which are called booses). Outside Swaledale, hay-lofts are the rule rather than the exception. Hay goes into the barn through a forking-hole, frequently in a gable wall but sometimes in the

▽ *Portrait of a Swaledale barn built around 1830*

38

rear wall, especially when a barn is built on a slope with the lower wall at the rear.

Single-bay barns accommodating four cows are between 24 and 32f long and about 16f wide. There are usually two doors in the front wall for farmer and cows, though smaller barns may have only a single door while larger ones have three. A two-bay barn is nearer 50f long and houses eight cows.

Most barns are floored with cobbles, with larger settle-stones along the outer end of the booses. Wall-slits allow ventilation to keep the hay dry and sweet. The walls themselves are two-skinned, with rubble between. Long stones called throughs run at right angles through both skins to tie the wall and strengthen the structure. Throughs were often left with projecting outer ends, contributing to the general rough-hewn, textural character of these simple yet functional buildings.

In the Craven area of Wharfedale, Littondale, Ribblesdale and around Malham, laithe barns are larger than elsewhere and have more architectural detail. Many have roofed porches to allow unloading of hay or corn under cover. Stone threshing-floors in line with the porch have the boses on either side. There are lean-to outshuts for calf-hulls, smaller ones for dog-kennels.

Handsome barns feature prominently in the village scene in the Craven region with Arncliffe, Grassington, Threshfield and Malham being particularly noteworthy.

△ *Barn porch, Wharfedale* △ *Shippon and hayloft, Swaledale*

Arnside Knott

Arnside Knott faces the Lake District across the Kent estuary at the north–east corner of Morecambe Bay. The Knott is a unique area of limestone crags and pavements dotted with scree slopes and glacial erratic boulders. There are several tracks and nature trails in the area; this variation gives walkers a good flavour of the limestone features and woodlands both young and old.

Car park: Arnside Knott (NT), 1m S of Arnside village, SW of Milnthorpe (on A6 N of Lancaster).
Grid ref: SD 449 773.

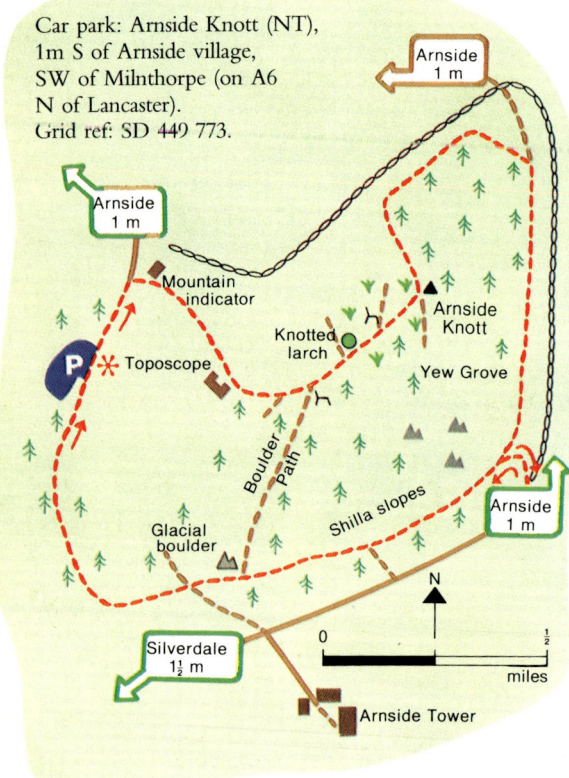

Arnside
1 m

Arnside
1 m

Mountain
indicator

P

Toposcope

Knotted
larch

Arnside
Knott

Yew Grove

Boulder Path

Shilla slopes

Glacial
boulder

Arnside
1 m

Silverdale
1½ m

N

0   ½
miles

Arnside Tower

The Knott, craggy with limestone but flat and partly wooded on top, supports an interesting selection of wildlife including rare ferns and grasses. This 3½m trail takes in many of the limestone features and there are good views from the toposcope and trig-point.

From the main car park entrance, walk back along the road a few yards to study the mountain indicator and the view it explains. From this point turn up the hill on either path, since both go to the toposcope. This is a more comprehensive mountain indicator; the stone walls support engraved steel plates which identify the Cumbrian Hills across the bay, Shap Fell and the Howgills to the east, and the Pennines and Bowland Fells to the south.

The long-lived yews at Arnside provide shelter and food, in the form of their bright red berries, for many creatures. The yew's extensive root system clings to the steepest slopes

Leave the toposcope and with the estuary on your
left take the path into the woodland past a fine beech.
Through the wood – a mixture of larch, oak, beech
and yew – there is wooded heathland where over a
hundred different flowering plants have been identified. Their blooms are particularly colourful in
autumn when the purples of marjoram and knapweed
contrast with masses of hawkweed, ragwort and
goldenrod.

A bench on the right marks the link with the
Boulder Path, a lower track round the Knott. This is
named after the large boulder (an 'erratic' deposited by
a long-melted glacier) on its route.

Farther on to the left there is an extraordinary
survivor of a Victorian larch plantation which was
felled during the First World War. This is the 'knotted
pine', in fact a long-dead larch, which stands like a
modern sculpture, pointing to the north and the high
hills. Since the larches were removed there has been
much natural regeneration and a wealth of shrubs and
trees grow on the Knott, including buckthorn, spindle,
box, barberry, juniper, beech, wild cherry and pine.

Past the knotted pine, at the bench between stone
uprights, take the path to the right that leads to the
triangulation pillar. This is the Knott's highest point,
522f, with fine views. From here, go down the left-
hand path until it meets a wall and stile, with open

△ *A solitary hawthorn in
flower on the outward section
through pasture*

▷ *Massed greenery of young
trees regenerating after
removal of the old larches*

pastures the other side. Turn right, keeping in the woodland with the wall to your left, on the path that leads to the Yew Grove. The many fine old yews in this area make an important contribution to the natural history of the Knott. The red berries from the female tree feed autumn flocks of mistle thrushes, blackbirds, fieldfares and redwings. The hard seeds go through the birds undigested and in winter greenfinches, bullfinches and a few hawfinches eat the kernels. Among these yews, at dusk on a warm evening, the woodcocks give their croaking call and the ghostly greenish lights of glow-worms shine from grass tussocks in the clearings.

The path is joined by the track from Arnside to Silverdale, then goes farther down the hill almost to the Silverdale road. It is worth descending to the stile and the road for a view to the right of Arnside Tower, an old pele tower built for border defences and now in ruins. Back on the path through the wood, to the right and above the road, the steep limestone crags of an old quarry tower over you. Through a gate the nature of

the slopes changes to fine scree, locally called shilla.
Rabbits live here and in the spring one or two pairs of
shelduck, easy to identify with their black, white and
chestnut plumage, search for nesting places in abandoned rabbit holes.

In the past these slopes have been badly eroded by
thoughtless visitors. The NT has planted the shilla with
parsley fern to stabilize it and strung lengths of
weighted net along the slope to catch falling stones.
Notices ask the public to keep off these slopes since
they are not only easily eroded but also dangerous.

Past the shilla slopes the track, now wider, goes
through woodland which provides cover for roe deer
and red squirrel. Ferns are well represented, from
bracken to the rare adder's-tongue. To the right,
climbing back to the toposcope, is Boulder Path.

All too soon you are at the car park again as the walk
comes full circle. Many visits are needed to appreciate
the unique quality of the limestone Knott, with its rare
flowers, moths and butterflies, interesting geological
formations and unsurpassed views.

△ ◁ A drystone wall on
the route; note the slanting
'capping' stones
◁ Familiar NT sign at the
entrance to woodland

△ In late spring and early
summer the woodland floor
is carpeted with shade-
tolerant plants such as dog's
mercury

Richmond & Hudswell

This wood-and-riverside ramble includes fine views of lower Swaledale and a visit to the picturesque North Yorkshire town of Richmond, with its imposing castle. Some paths are steep and can be muddy in wet weather.

The green at Richmond is the start of this 4m walk on an elongated figure-8 through Hudswell, Billybank and Calfhall Woods. Be warned – the track tends to be muddy and slippery after rain. There is an alternative smaller car park at the foot of Cravengate, almost on the green. From the Victoria Road car park turn right, then left along Cravengate to reach the start.

Cross Bargate Green to Richmond Green Bridge, over the River Swale. Historically, Bargate and Bargate Green were medieval suburbs of Richmond outside the fourteenth-century walls; the hillside above the small car park to the west was called Tenter Bank on an early eighteenth-century map, suggesting that woollen cloth was manufactured in this part of the town. The octagonal building on the hill is Culloden

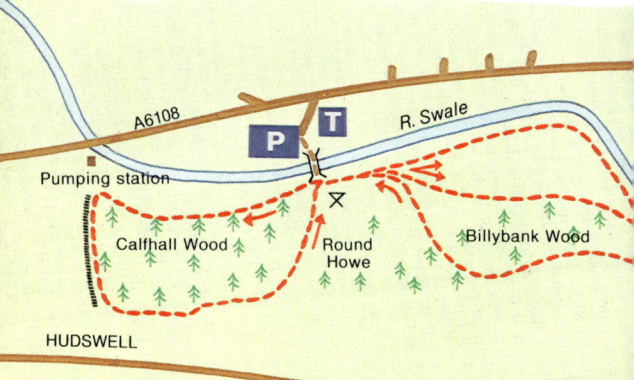

Tower, built by John Yorke in 1746 to mark the Hanoverian victory which also ensured Whig supremacy in parliament. Yorke was one of two MPs representing Richmond, and his mansion occupied a riverside site below the small car park until the early eighteenth century. The Tower is owned by the Landmark Trust. To the east is the town and the imposing Richmond Castle.

Cross the Swale by John Carr's bridge of 1789, which replaced the older one. Note the stone panel in the centre of the eastern (downstream) parapet that gives distances to Askrigg and Lancaster. The Richmond-Lancaster Turnpike was created in 1751 and crossed the river at this point.

Over the river and immediately beyond the first stone cottage at the bottom of Sleegill, turn right up stone steps and on to a good track that climbs steeply into Billybank Wood. After about 300y a short stretch of stone flags leads to a stile, with three yellow waymarks on a post beyond it. Keep along the top of the wood, passing many holly trees on the right. After 100y turn right over a stile into the wood and, with a gully on your left, descend to some rustic railings and a small wooden bridge. Cross and follow a good track through the woods, where a stand of tall pines contrasts with the dominant deciduous trees. In late May and early June the woods here are richly carpeted

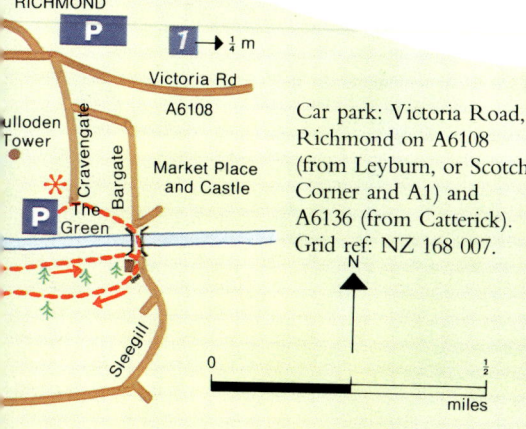

RICHMOND

Victoria Rd
A6108

Market Place
and Castle

ulloden
Tower

Cravengate
Bargate

The
Green

Sleegill

Car park: Victoria Road, Richmond on A6108 (from Leyburn, or Scotch Corner and A1) and A6136 (from Catterick). Grid ref: NZ 168 007.

N

0   ½
miles

47

with bluebells and ramsons (wild garlic).

Beyond a fallen pine the path descends sharply, hairpins to the right and left, and reaches a stile at the foot of a barbed-wire fence. Keep to the upper track which undulates through the wood, narrowing between two wooden fences, with glimpses down to the right of cliff faces that are a favourite nesting-place for jackdaws. At its end the twin-fenced path drops steeply to a level field opposite a caravan site. Ahead is the NT Picnic Site, identified by the NT sign. A metal footbridge spans the river to a car park on the north bank, adjoining the Richmond-Leyburn road.

To the south is the appropriately-named Round Howe, a tree-covered mound showing new plantings of deciduous and coniferous trees. This is part of the NT's Hudswell Wood. Stay on the Swale's south bank and continue westwards along a good path, rising slightly and then dropping back to the riverside. Subsequently the path undulates and winds through Calfhall Wood for about 1m, when you reach the

▷ *Steep, rocky parts of the Swale valley are occupied in spring by nesting jackdaws. This cheeky bird may pluck wool for its nest lining from the backs of distracted sheep*
◁ *John Yorke's Culloden Tower*
▽ *An interesting study of conifers in Billybank Woods*

49

△ *A V-and-step stile on the path through Calfhall Woods. This design is a combination of the standard 3-bar-and-step stile familiar to all country walkers. The upper ends of the V are extended beyond the cross-bars to provide handgrips*
▷ *The River Swale flows over its stony bed on the way to Richmond, then to join the Ure and the Ouse near York before emptying into the Humber estuary*

Pumping Station. The path emerges from the wood and a series of steps climbs steeply up the hill to the left (south). These were made by German prisoners in the Second World War, to link the Pumping Station to another treatment plant at the top of the hill, near Hudswell village. There are 328 steps – but you need climb only 295 to where a prominent track (*Footpath* sign) crosses the flight. Pause to regain breath and look back for the view of lower Swaledale, with Whitcliffe Scar and Willance's Leap prominent across the valley.

Turn left from the steps and head east; where the track forks, keep left and enter the top of Calfhall Wood. You soon leave the trees by a stile at the top of some steps, walk the length of a field and return to the wood in less than 100y. About ½m from the top of the steps the field path from Hudswell village joins by a gate and a NT sign. The 'finger' of NT land here is

unwooded, and a rough track follows it diagonally into the valley between Calfhall Wood and Round Howe and back to the familiar Picnic Site. Past the picnickers, take the well-defined riverside path eastwards to emerge from hawthorn and blackthorn into a riverside meadow. Here you have a choice: a riverside path to the left, or a track that hugs the woods to your right. These routes converge at the end of the field, where Billybank Wood comes down to the river.

Cross a stile into the wood, where a good path rises slightly at first and then drops slowly to take you back to the cottage at the foot of Sleegill. Alternatively, if the river is low and you have enough energy, there is a boulder-hopping route along the Swale's south bank which eventually joins the woodland path 150y west of Richmond Bridge. Across the bridge, left at the green, and the car park and town comforts are ahead.

Gowbarrow Fell

A walk of great variety and beauty through
the NT property of Gowbarrow Park. The
route displays wildlife, woodland, wildflowers,
the spectacular Aira Force waterfall and the
panorama of Ullswater and its
surrounding fells.

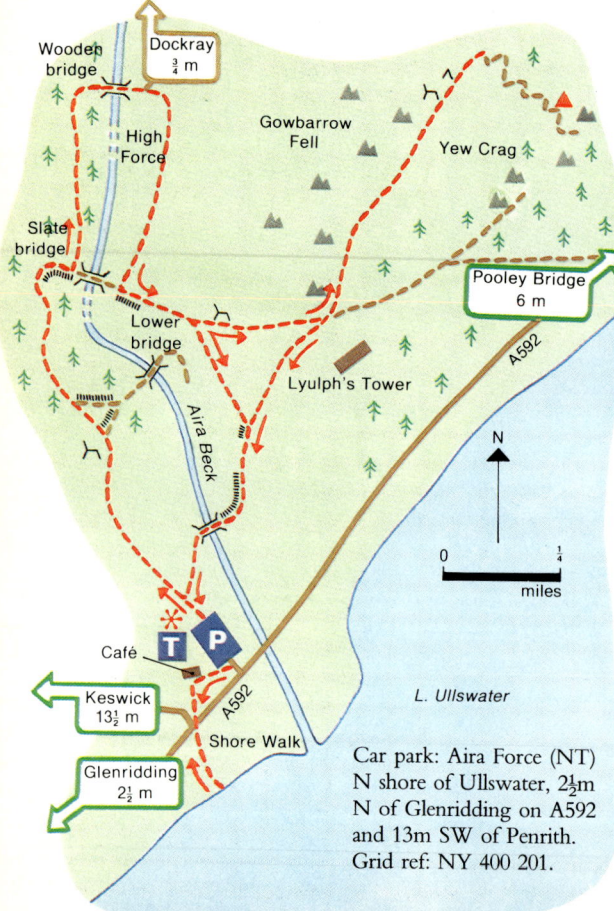

Wooden bridge

Dockray
¾ m

High Force

Gowbarrow Fell

Yew Crag

Slate bridge

Lower bridge

Pooley Bridge
6 m

Aira Beck

Lyulph's Tower

A592

N

0   ¼
miles

Café

*

T   P

Keswick
13½ m

A592

Shore Walk

Glenridding
2½ m

L. Ullswater

Car park: Aira Force (NT)
N shore of Ullswater, 2½m
N of Glenridding on A592
and 13m SW of Penrith.
Grid ref: NY 400 201.

This 4½m ramble through Gowbarrow Park (once a medieval deer park) is particularly rewarding since it gives those who follow its path ideas of where further explorations could be continued on another visit. There are tremendous views of Ullswater, particularly from Yew Crag. It is essential to have good maps because the paths, though clear, are numerous and it is all too easy to take the wrong one.

Leave the Aira Force car park through the wicket gate opposite the road entrance and take the path well to the left of the Aira Beck. This is Park Brow – pasture land dotted with newly-planted deciduous trees. Before going through the gate into the woods above Aira Glen, it is worth looking back at the head of Ullswater and at High Street to the left, on whose heights there is a Roman road. A few yards into the wood a path and a series of steps to the right bring into sight the spectacular 65f-high waterfall plunging from beneath a slate bridge. On sunny days when there is plenty of stream and spray, a rainbow curves across the sparkling water. The shaded and water-splashed rock face makes a good home for interesting mosses, lichens and ferns.

There is a legend that while the knight Sir Eglamore was absent at the Crusades, his betrothed Lady took to sleep-walking in this Glen. On his return his joyous cry of greeting woke her too suddenly and she fell to her death down the dark, rocky slopes. The legend inspired Wordsworth to write a poem, *The Somnambulist*.

In the Glen itself there are many fine old oaks, wych elm, hazel and ash, Douglas fir, pine and exotic trees. The small bird population is also varied and includes treecreeper, nuthatch and spotted flycatcher. Leaving the fall and returning to the left bank of Aira Glen, the path goes up past the slate bridge at the head of the fall to the upper section of the Force. Here the Glen is wider with several small waterfalls in Aira Beck; ancient oaks line the banks and the wren-like dipper can be seen bobbing and curtseying on the rocks in the stream. High Force, the waterfall at the top of Aira Glen, has rock walls 20f high with moss cover. The well-wooded banks provide good living for the red squirrel.

Cross the wooden bridge beyond the fall and follow

△ *Looking back down Aira Glen*
▷ *The spectacular Aira Force falls (force is an Old Norse term for waterfall)*

△ *The dipper seeks food in fast-flowing streams like Aira Beck*

the path up the bank where there are new steps of local stone, to return south along the other side of the Glen. (For those who wish to explore farther up Aira Beck the path goes $\frac{3}{4}$m to Dockray village where good timing will land you a pub lunch.) Keep to the top path above the stream and follow it down to the slate bridge – an unusual feature since wooden bridges are the norm. Here you can see the cataract from above. The newly-grassed area beside the bridge is part of the NT's extensive erosion-repair work around Aira Beck.

After climbing the bank again the path divides. The right fork continues down the Glen and finally crosses

the Beck over a wooden bridge to return to the car park. The left fork, leading towards a stile over a fence, is your path to Yew Crag on Gowbarrow Fell. This is a climb of nearly a mile, but a most rewarding viewpoint for those who find heights exhilarating.

Once over the stile, follow the path above the fence round the shoulder of the fell. Below, near the shore of the lake, is the castellated hunting lodge called Lyulph's Tower. For centuries this land was the property of the Howards of Greystoke and there is a tradition that Lyulph, first Baron of Greystoke, put a hunting lodge there. The present Lyulph's Tower was built on the same site in 1780 as a shooting box for the Earl of Surrey, afterwards Duke of Norfolk.

The path climbs the fell at a long angle towards the distant Yew Crag, and soon the three reaches of Ullswater – a double dog's-leg – come into view. This lake, $7\frac{1}{2}$m long, is considered by many to be the most beautiful of the English lakes, with its head in the high fells and its outflow in the Eamont valley. Trout and perch live in the glaciated valley beneath its surface along with a unique fish called the schelly, a type of powan isolated here after the ice age and now different from its relatives in other lakes.

The first length of path is narrow with a sharp slope down to the right, but later it eases and you can walk and enjoy the view. Above Yew Crag there is a welcome bench with the Pennines visible to the north-east. The Crag, approximately 700f high, is an outcrop of the underlying Borrowdale Volcanic Series. An excellent variety of shrubs and trees grow on the crags and scree, including small-leaved lime, juniper, yew, oak, alder and hawthorn. In the woods below and on

the fell sides, all part of a site registered by the British Trust for Ornithology, are red grouse, woodcock, ring ousel, whinchat and long-tailed tit. Woodland flowers include grass of parnassus and bird's-eye primrose, a local northern species. Above the crag you may see a buzzard or kestrel gliding in the thermals.

There is a route south down Yew Crag but it is steep, dangerous and not recommended. Return on the same path as your ascent, which affords even better views on the way back. Rejoin the Aira Force path to your left down a short flight of steps near the lower bridge, and the car park is only a few minutes away. Outside the car park is the NT Cafe and Shop, built of local materials to blend with the landscape.

There are many other paths to enjoy on Gowbarrow Fell and in the Park, including a walk across the road to the lakeshore. It was near here that William Wordsworth and his sister Dorothy saw the wild daffodils; Dorothy wrote, 'I never saw daffodils so beautiful', her brother was tempted to write his famous poem *Daffodils*: 'I wandered lonely as a cloud...'

△ *Looking east over Ullswater from the summit of Yew Crag*
◁ △ *The unusual slate bridge above Aira Force*
◁ *Long Crag looms above Ullswater, on route to Yew Crag*

Brimham & Riva Hill

The spectacular Brimham Rocks, near Ripon, are formations of millstone grit eroded into extraordinary shapes by the elements. The walk winds across open moor, grazed farmland with prolific hedgerows, and woods of ash and sycamore before arriving at the rock formations.

Brimham and the surrounding area provide easy walking country with fine views, the contrast of moor and wood, and the fantastic shapes of Brimham Rocks as a finale to this $4\frac{1}{2}$m route.

After parking, return to the entrance and 50y past the ticket-collector's hut take a right into a farm track and past the NT sign for a splendid view of Nidderdale. About 20y before the gate turn left on to a short grassy track and cross the road to a gravelly path (*NT No Riders* sign). This leads to an open moor of

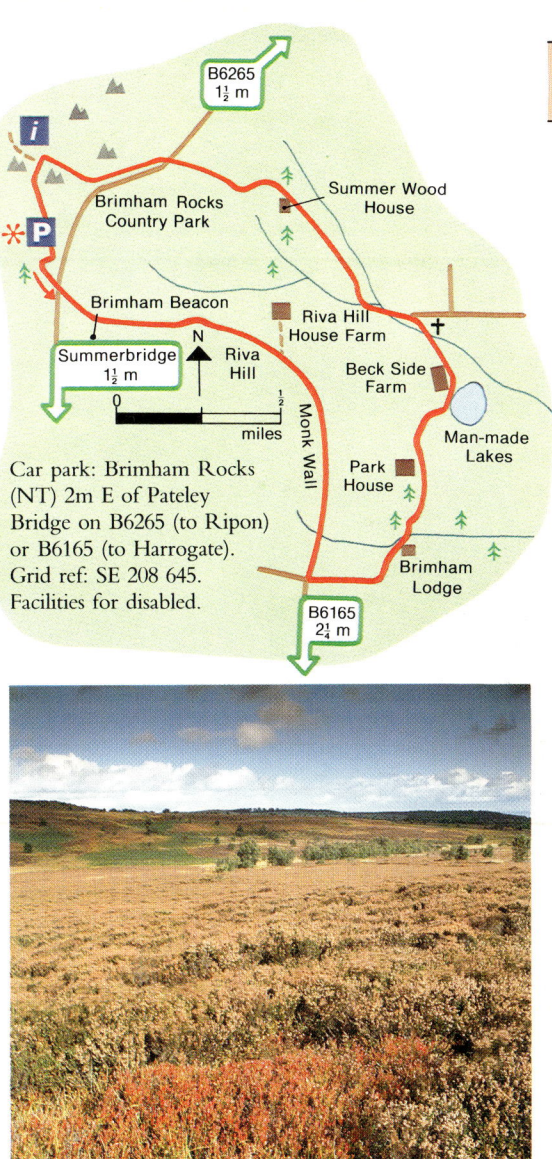

B6265
1½ m

Summer Wood
House

Brimham Rocks
Country Park

P

Brimham Beacon

Riva Hill
House Farm

Summerbridge
1½ m

N

Riva
Hill

0   ½
miles

Beck Side
Farm

Man-made
Lakes

Monk Wall

Park
House

Brimham
Lodge

Car park: Brimham Rocks
(NT) 2m E of Pateley
Bridge on B6265 (to Ripon)
or B6165 (to Harrogate).
Grid ref: SE 208 645.
Facilities for disabled.

B6165
2¼ m

△ The open moorland on the approach to Riva Hill
◁ The 'over-the-shoulder' view of Brimham Rocks

*Bell heather is one of
our three main heather
species, with petals fused into
a bell-shaped corolla tube; it
flowers from June to
September*

heather (beautiful in August), bilberry, small silver
birches and rowan. About $\frac{3}{4}$m ahead is the dark hump
of Riva Hill, with the rocks of Brimham Beacon to the
south and closer. As you approach Riva Hill the path
reaches a stone wall with a *NT Boundary* sign by the
gate. Go through the gate on to a grassy track with a
stone wall on your left and to the right the moor
studded with gorse bushes.

Past Riva Hill House farm entrance follow the
concrete track to reveal pleasant farm and woodland
views north and north-east. After 200y keep right,
passing a cattle trough in the wall ahead. At the next
gate, 200y later, the wall beyond and to the left is built
of nicely-squared stones. Swing slightly right to head
south and follow the lane for $\frac{1}{2}$m to the metalled road.
Monk Wall joins this lane on the left; admire its
medieval squared masonry. The wall marks the
boundary of Brimham Lodge, the former Fountains
Abbey grange.

When you reach the metalled road turn left on to a
good farm track and 400y later left again towards
Brimham Lodge. The track passes between farm

△ *Common heather (ling)*
has petals more separate
than bell heather
Bilberry, a low shrub ▷

△ *Typical wall-and-moor Dales country near Riva Hill*

△ Brimham Lodge, the former grange (country house) of Fountains Abbey. Rebuilt in 1661 it is three-storeyed, with mullioned windows and ornamental stonework (finials) to its turrets

▷ The pond near Beck Side Farm, about two-thirds of the way along the walk. Such man-made stretches of water are oases in moorland areas like Brimham, where the natural moor bogs and ponds are too acidic to support food suitable for the local wildfowl population

▽ One of the few wooded sections on the walk, near Beck Side Farm

buildings and through a wide gate down a short hill winding among sycamores. Swing right by a small larch and fir plantation in a tiny valley, then left with Park House appearing ahead; beyond the buildings the track becomes a double-walled lane.

The pleasing lane ends at three gates. Enter the right one into a field and keep a stone wall close to your left. Exit the field through another gate, turn left (keeping the wall on your left) and pause to survey the small man-made lakes with their waterfowl to the right. Ahead is Beck Side Farm, where you go diagonally left and then slightly right through a timber yard. It looks private but the right of way descends to a small plantation where a beck (stream) emerges as a waterfall from a former millpond, now ornamental. Continue

past a modern bungalow to a lane with a former chapel prominent on the corner (look behind it for the Victorian pillar box). Keeping left, walk down a slight hill and over a cattle grid to a beck in the small wood. After another 70y fork right as directed by the yellow waymark arrow on a tree. Ignore a similar arrow by the next gate on the left and keep to the woodland lane as it swings right and left. Cross the beck at a ford and wind up the hill for 200y to pass through a gate at the summit, where the wood ends.

With the hawthorn and holly hedge on your left, head for Summer Wood House (waymark arrow by the gate), and follow the concrete drive by the house

up to a cattle grid. Brimham Rocks appear at last and the concrete way ahead is clear. Another cattle grid and you are back on NT land.

Turn left at the road and in 350y, after the road bends and starts to dip, choose the well-defined track leading to the right. Soon Brimham House (now the NT Information Centre) is in view but disappears as the track winds through birches, heather and bilberry past the weird rock formations. In $\frac{1}{4}$m you meet the main Brimham Rocks track below the House, and a short detour allows you to browse in the Information Centre or the children to scramble on the rocks. Finally turn left and the car park is less than 400y away.

△ One of Brimham Rocks' 'erratics', boulders left isolated from their fellows when the ice melted long ago

◁ In times gone by the land of Brimham Rocks was a free-for-all, with cars parked anywhere and everywhere, and human erosion threatening the very existence of the weird and wonderful nature-sculpted sandstones. In 1976 the NT completed a car park to control car access, and restoration work was carried out on Brimham House and the areas around the rocks. Some of the lost dignity and quietness have now returned to Brimham Moor

Malham & Janet's Foss

This walk is in famous limestone country around Malham, near Skipton in the south Dales. The route passes through meadow, along a limestone gorge to the waterfall at Janet's Foss, over rough fells with panoramic views, and joins the long-distance Pennine Way footpath for its last half-mile.

Malhamdale is justly famous for its beautiful scenery. This 5½m trail takes the walker along the limestone scarp of the Mid-Craven Fault to Weets Top and over Hanlith Moor for spectacular views of the dale, Gordale Scar, Malham Cove and the surrounding craggy countryside. For another route in this spectacular landscape see walk 16.

Leave the car park, turn left past the National Park Information Centre and follow the road towards the village. In 100y cross Malham Beck (stream) by a clapper bridge near a small stone building, turn right

△ *Conscientious walkers keep in single file over pasture*

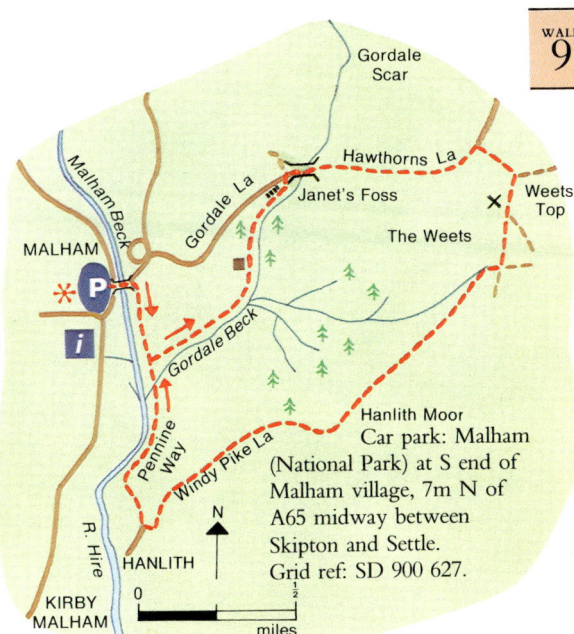

Car park: Malham (National Park) at S end of Malham village, 7m N of A65 midway between Skipton and Settle. Grid ref: SD 900 627.

by the beck and cross a stile where the National Park notice board states: *Footpath through meadows, Single file please, Your feet are killing me!*

The loose, stony path beyond crosses one ladder stile after 100y, and a second after another 200y where a signpost points out the Pennine Way and Janet's Foss. Follow the latter (you will return, hopefully, by the former).

Keep left of Mires Barn and follow the waymark signs, crossing more ladder stiles. The signpost *Gordale* points your way past a large, splendidly-shaped ash on the right; the limestone wall on the left has huge boulders along its base and smaller rounded ones above, representing field-clearance from a glacial or stream-bed origin. New Laithe, on the left, is a fine example of the laithe (porched barn) characteristic of the Malham area. The large laithe doors usually open on to a flagged cart stand; during previous centuries, when corn was grown locally, the flagged floors inside were used for threshing and winnowing. The other

△ *The elm, its leaf and fruit*

▽ *In shady Janet's Foss valley, plants cloak the limestone scars*

bays housed cattle-stalls below with timber balks supporting hay-mow lofts above.

The path crosses a ladder stile by New Laithe (notice the owl hole high in the barn's gable wall), follows Gordale Beck to its right and enters woodland by a sign *NT Janet's Foss*. The NT owns this 7½a wooded limestone gorge, also known as Little Gordale, and the path runs its length. The wood is an important conservation area, with sycamore, ash, beech, wych elm and hawthorn over a dense and varied ground cover. Dead timber provides a habitat for various insects; dippers and kingfishers frequent the stream, and the green woodpecker is here but is more likely to be heard than seen. *Please* keep to the footpath.

A few limestone steps at the end of the gorge reveal the waterfall of Janet's Foss. Gordale Beck tumbles over the tufa screen, an apron of petrified moss formed by the deposition of mineral salts dissolved in the falling water. In the eighteenth century a small cave by the fall was inhabited by smelters from the copper mines on Pikedaw Hill, near Malham. A narrow rocky pass leads from Janet's Foss to Gordale Lane a few yards away, with the spectacular limestone gorge of Gordale Scar beyond. Gordale Lane offers a one-mile return to Malham by turning left, but this walk continues eastwards with a steep ¾m climb up the metalled Hawthorns Lane. At the top, turn right by an iron sign *Public Bridleway* and, still climbing, along a walled and very stony lane to arrive at Weets Top (1,350f). Weets Cross, in the angle of two walls, is

△ *Sheep-cropped turf of the limestone plateau, Hanlith*

△ △ *Upland Dales scene, through a wall that needs attention*
△ *The infant River Aire flanks the Pennine Way*
▷ *Horse chestnuts display their 'candles' of flowers*

probably medieval in origin and most likely a boundary mark on the Fountains Abbey estate.

Go through a gate to the open moor, and follow the signpost *Windy Pike Lane* (1m). Descend gradually to a ladder stile at a wall corner, and take the track signposted *Hanlith*. This continues south-west across the rough fell pasture of Hanlith Moor, its course picked out by yellow-topped wooden waymark posts. Follow them steadily downhill, appreciating the wide panorama dominated by Pendle Hill in the distance. To your right Gordale Scar and the limestone landscape of the Mid-Craven Fault come into view.

At the bottom of Hanlith Moor a gate gives access to

Windy Pike Lane, double walled with dark sandstone
and gritstone, and this descends steadily past a conifer
plantation on the right to Hanlith. By now the walls
are limestone again. A steep right hairpin leads to a
farmhouse with rendered walls. Turn right and you
are on the Pennine Way with a sign pointing your
route to the right of the farm, into meadows. Yellow
waymarks and more *Pennine Way* signs clearly
indicate the easy track, over a succession of stiles, to
Mires Barn and other landmarks familiar from the
beginning of the walk. Ahead, beyond Malham
village, is Malham Cove itself – the final flourish in
Britain's most spectacular limestone landscape.

Beatrix Potter

In her will the authoress and illustrator Beatrix Potter bequeathed to the NT 15 farms, many cottages and 4,000a of land. She wanted to make sure her 'dear farms and sheep' were cared for after her death; giving them to the NT seemed to her the best way.

Beatrix Potter first heard about the NT through Hardwicke Rawnsley, later one of its founders in the

△ *Hill Top, Beatrix Potter's home during her writing period, is a typical seventeenth-century Lakes farmhouse*

Lake District. Rawnsley was vicar of Wray, on Windermere, when her parents took her to Wray Castle for a holiday – she was 16 at the time. Hardwicke's warm personality made him a welcome visitor and they were friends until his death in 1920.

In her mid-30s Beatrix thought she might venture on a book, *The Tale of Peter Rabbit*, and she asked Hardwicke for advice. On his suggestion she submitted the completed work to Frederick Warne and Co, but only after she published it at her own expense and it proved successful were the publishers convinced. The enormous sales of *Peter Rabbit* made it possible for Beatrix, in 1905, to buy Hill Top Farm, in Near Sawrey. She thought of farm life as immensely satisfying and she liked the countryside round Hawkshead; later she was to speak of it as 'a pleasant peaceful foreground of the hills, I think more liable to be spoilt than the fells themselves'.

As her book royalties increased she bought more farms to satisfy her need to own some of this countryside. Her marriage in 1913 to William Heelis, a local solicitor, marked the end of her writing and illustrating life. From then on Mrs William Heelis, as she preferred to be called, became a farmer.

As the years went by she purchased more properties, her husband advising. Her biggest purchase was in 1930, when she bought the 4,000a Monk Coniston estate to prevent it from being broken up. She then offered to sell half to the NT at cost, retaining the rest with a promise to leave it to the NT in her will. This offer was gratefully accepted and money was raised for land which included much of Little Langdale, Tilberthwaite and Tarn Hows. Mrs Heelis was asked to continue managing this on the NT's behalf until a suitable land agent was found. She held the job until 1936, just seven years before her death.

Beatrix Potter was one of the first of many benefactors who left their farms and estates to be cared for by the NT. In the north-west 85 farms and 140,000a of land, over a quarter of the Lake District National Park, are now protected. The bequests include some of the most spectacular scenery in the Lakes, but also the gentle hills and small farms of the countryside around Hawkshead and Sawrey – Beatrix Potter's gift to the nation.

Hawkshead

An interesting but not too demanding walk through the placid countryside west of Lake Windermere. The gentle hills, wooded valleys and small hamlets have historic connections with William Wordsworth and Beatrix Potter.

Hawkshead, the start of the 5¾m walk, is the old market town for the mild landscape between Lake Windermere and the head of Coniston Water – land once described by Beatrix Potter as 'the most pleasant country in the world'. The rounded hills ('drumlins' left by glacier action), unexpected tarns, peaceful lowlands and ancient architecture make the walk delightfully varied. A visit to the NT Information Centre and Shop just off the main square will provide more information on the area and its associations with Wordsworth and Mrs Heelis (Beatrix Potter).

Leave Hawkshead car park by the village entrance and opposite, across the street, are the gates to Hawkshead grammar school. The path is signposted and goes past this school, open to the public, where William Wordsworth was a pupil from 1778 to 1787; the desk on which he carved his name is still there. Next comes the churchyard, where yew trees shelter lichened gravestones. As you leave the village, look

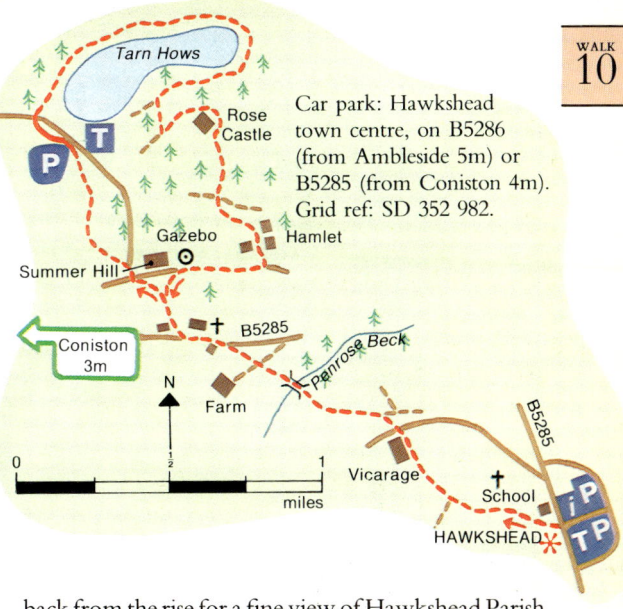

Tarn Hows

Rose Castle

Car park: Hawkshead town centre, on B5286 (from Ambleside 5m) or B5285 (from Coniston 4m). Grid ref: SD 352 982.

Gazebo

Hamlet

Summer Hill

Coniston 3m

B5285

Penrose Beck

N

Farm

B5285

0   ½   1

miles

Vicarage

School

HAWKSHEAD

back from the rise for a fine view of Hawkshead Parish Church. A broad rectangular building with a square tower at its western end, the church stands in a commanding position on the crown of an oval-shaped hillock. Up to 1875 it was whitewashed and in *The Prelude* Wordsworth says: 'I saw the snow-white church upon her hill, Sit like a throned lady sending out a gracious look all over her domain.'

From the churchyard the path is fenced on one side for a short length with the slabs of slate that often indicate a parish boundary. A right fork signed *Tarn Hows* leads past the vicarage, a relatively modern white house, then to a lane where in the warmer months pink purslane and wild garlic fight for a place alongside the wall. A turn left and another quickly right reveal open parkland, with a gently rising path up Hawkshead Hill and opening views of the Fairfield range ahead. To the right the line of Claife Heights culminates in Latterbarrow, crowned by a stone monument kept in good repair by the NT – though careful research has failed to discover what it commemorates.

◁ *An over-the-shoulder view of Hawkshead, showing the Church and stone-slab fence flanking the route's path*

$\triangle$ *Wild thyme*

$\triangleleft$ *Speedwell*

$\triangleleft$ *Rose Castle, passed on the start of the return section*
$\triangledown$ *The upland lake of Tarn Hows, bought for the NT by Sir H Scott; the purchase was made possible by Mrs Heelis (Beatrix Potter)*

△ *Heath milkwort*

◁ *Heath bedstraw*

Tormentil ▷

Past the maple trees and wellingtonia the route is by the higher, left-hand path. At the top of the parkland area cross the bridge in the wooded valley carved by Penrose Beck. Below the beck the bridge falls steeply into a miniature rocky gill where natural vegetation, including rare mosses and ferns, grows luxuriantly in the green shade.

Beyond the gill are farm fields; cross a farm road and take the signed path, which ends in a stile in a wall. Over the stile is the Tarn Hows road, and you turn left for Hawkshead Hill hamlet. This outpost village, seeming to look down on Hawkshead and its association with trade, is mainly a mixture of seventeenth-century vernacular cottages and small houses.

Take the next road to the right, which bears left and soon joins the main Ambleside road at Summer Hill Cottage, a guest house. The route is now left on to the main road, then right past the side of the guest house to Tarn Hows.

In a few yards you escape from the road on to NT land by turning left to cross a stile opposite an unfortunate rubbish tip. At first the way is along the side of the road wall, but *PATH* painted on a boulder nudges walkers across slightly more boggy land to the next stile. In this upland pasture the sheep recline on rocky knolls, wearing expressions of aloof indifference; the vegetation is rich in small plants and herbs such as tormentil, heath bedstraw, milkwort, speedwell and thyme. Yellow wagtails catch the eye with their flickering flight and a raucous laugh in the woods announces the green woodpecker. Ahead are the first views of the Coniston Fells.

The path reaches a field corner where you turn right over the wall into a wood. A climb through trees past a small slate quarry brings the road into sight but the path goes parallel to it, along the wall, to emerge opposite the car park. Pause here to enjoy the glorious panorama of the Tarn and the fells around it. With the map out and working westwards (left to right) the view embraces Coniston Water, then Coniston Fells, Wetherlam, Bowfells, the Langdale Pikes and – on a good day – Helvellyn, Fairfield and Red Screes. It is beautiful at any season of the year, with a changing richness of colour. A specially widened gate and short, level path allow wheelchair visitors to reach a point where there is another aspect of these hills.

Downhill now, avoid the road again by taking a path over grass to the left. The route follows the clockwise circuit of Tarn Hows. Start by crossing Glen Mary at the dam which created Tarn Hows by turning three unassuming ponds into the splendid stretch of water it is today. The NT's erosion repair on the path has been successful but much maintenance is still required to cope with the 500,000 visitors who come to the area each year. Bullfinches look hopefully for picnickers along the woodside path, and in spring a mist of bluebells lies between the trees and primroses peer from hollows. Pine, birch, oak and hazel close in on the path but there are still glimpses of water. Coot, moorhen and mallard have their homes here all year; greylag geese sometimes visit in the spring while red-breasted merganser and golden-eye come in the winter.

The path curves round the end of the tarn, and after two-thirds of the circuit a left fork leads up the fell to Rose Castle. Despite its name there are no ancient battlements, only a gamekeeper's small stone cottage. The path goes round to the front of the cottage and then takes a line from the gate left across a field, losing itself in the grass. The route is due south between two conifer plantations which clamp like pincers at a stile where the path appears again. Across the forestry road there is an iron gate which leads to a narrow lane.

△ △ *Pine roots search for anchorage in the thin soil*
△ *Looking down on Tarn Hows, with high fells at the back*

Latterbarrow with its anonymous monument comes
into view again and the lane opens into a small hamlet
with glimpses of lovely gardens. Continue to the cattle
grid and the road, then a right turn and you are back at
Summer Hill Cottage. The Hawkshead road is to the
left, opposite an unusual gazebo, and you turn into it to
retrace the first section of the walk. Take this further
opportunity to enjoy the views.

Back in Hawkshead there is a variety of refreshments and plenty of historical interest. As well as the
church and school, there are many seventeenth-
century cottages of great character.

East Witton

A pleasant, relaxing walk that undulates through the tranquil scenery of heather moor, pasture and arable land in Coverdale, south of Leyburn. On the way it passes Braithwaite Hall, a NT property (open only by appointment).

The mild and peaceful scenery of Coverdale is the basis of this moderate 6½m walk that passes the NT properties of Braithwaite Moor and Hall. The route is easy walking but finding it can be awkward, so good maps are essential. Braithwaite Hall, dating from 1667, is an occupied farmhouse and open for visits only by appointment with the tenants.

Park in East Witton village, preferably at the western end where the walk starts and finishes. (There is more space and shade on the eastern side but this adds almost ½m to the route.)

Turn left at the west end of the village, passing across the edge of a farmyard and through two gates. Take a right beyond the third, metal, gate with a fence on your right and open pasture to the left. In 200y pass through a gate at the bottom end of a cross wall

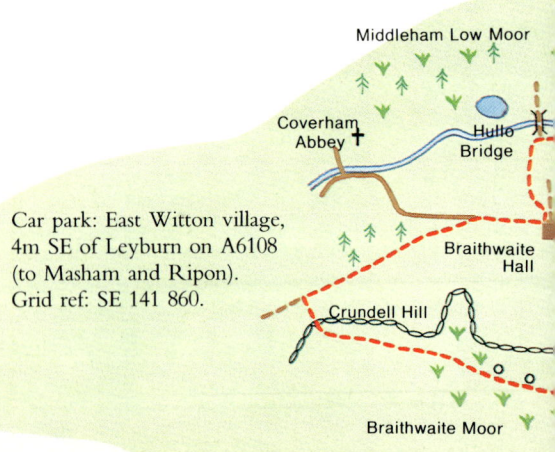

Middleham Low Moor

Coverham Abbey ✝

Hulla Bridge

Car park: East Witton village, 4m SE of Leyburn on A6108 (to Masham and Ripon). Grid ref: SE 141 860.

Braithwaite Hall

Crundell Hill

Braithwaite Moor

△ *The pretty Coverdale village of East Witton*

coming down the hillside, and the track starts climbing Witton Banks. In 250y swing upwards and bear left across a pasture, the way indicated by ridges in the grass. These soon identify the track as a slightly 'hollow way', rising to a wooden gate ahead.

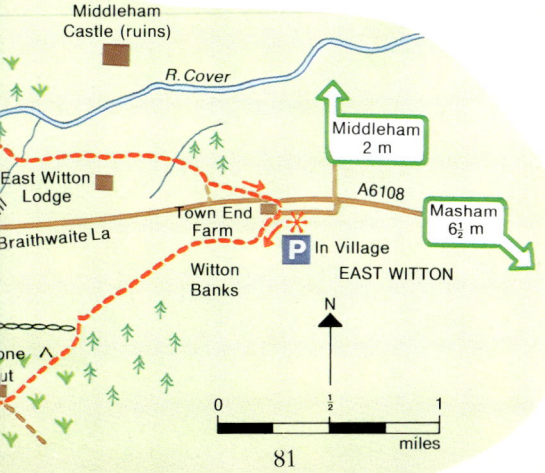

Continue climbing steadily towards the north-west corner of a conifer plantation, where there are two gates at right angles. Take the left one. From the angle between the gates the moor wall stretches away westwards, dividing enclosed pastures to the north from the open heather of Braithwaite Moor to the south. For the next 1½m the walk is out on this moor. A landmark to the west is Pen Hill, whose plateau-like summit ends sharply at its northern edge in a scarp face. Down in the valley to the north are the ruins of Middleham Castle.

Set out across the moor on an alignment that bisects the angle between the moor wall and the edge of the plantation. Soon you should be able to pick out a narrow path through the heather and bracken, and ahead is a stone pillar on an ancient burial mound. The column is probably a boundary-stone, and a very sketchy track keeps about 50y to its left. Keep south-

◁ *Hedged arable land dominates the scenery looking north across Coverdale*
▷ *The stone pillar set on a tumulus (barrow) on Braithwaite Moor; it probably marks an earlier boundary*
▽ *The NT's Braithwaite Hall, acquired in 1941, is open only by appointment*

west as best you can and aim for a derelict stone hut by old bell pits. These are circular hollows left by an old method of working coal a few feet below the surface. Spoil from a central shaft and its radiating circle of tunnels below was brought to the surface, and left as circular mounds surrounding the pits. These spoil-heaps are bare and some contain pieces of coal.

The way ahead remains indistinct, going west-north-west between the first and second of a row of shooting-butts, hopping from one bell-pit heap to the next. There are four pits altogether, roughly at 200y intervals, and the northern end of Pen Hill is a distant sighting point. Eventually you lose height and see a corner of the moor wall where it starts to go downhill. In the distance, across lower Coverdale, is Middleham Low Moor with its pond and trees by Ever Bank. The heather moor is now left behind.

Keep westwards, with a low defile (narrow, banked

path) on your right separating the now recognizable path from elongated Cundell Hill to the north. The path soon joins a wall coming in from the right. Keep to the north of this, enjoying views to Coverham Abbey and its farm across the River Cover to the right. Descend to the next wall corner, go through the right-hand of two gates, and keeping generally right head north-west across a field, aiming for (but not reaching) a long barn. Go through two more gates and aim for the upper side of a small conifer plantation. By now you are heading east-north-east; lower Coverdale is to your left and the hills you have crossed and descended are to your right. Continue across the low remains of a stone wall, then bear slightly left to join Braithwaite Lane (metalled) about $\frac{1}{4}$m west of Braithwaite Hall.

Immediately opposite the Hall's entrance drive and impressive north face (note NT sign) turn left through a field gate and follow a farm track north towards the River Cover at Hullo Bridge. Make a short detour to see the river flowing between wooded banks over a limestone bed with many potholes. Backtrack for the route to East Witton, which keeps the top of the slope to its south. Go through a broken wall, between trees, and follow the slope with a post and wire fence on your

△ The skylark's song is a
potent reminder of moors and
open grasslands
▷ The Cover's potholed bed
◁ Hullo Bridge spans the
Cover

right. At the end of the fence cross a small gully to a
little wooden gate and once through this follow the
left-hand edge of a large field, swinging right by Red
Bank Gill and turning your back on the River Cover.
Cross the tree-trunk bridge and look for a yellow
waymark on a fence about 50y below a dead elm, near
an ash and a sycamore. Cross the fence here; keep
another wooden fence on your right and in 100y go
through a gate on the right, by an ash tree, then left.
Note the hawthorn trees cut and shaped in the fence.

Keep the fence on your left, and where a sturdy oak
stands isolated in the field turn slightly away from the
fence and aim for a hedge corner 150y ahead (another
yellow waymark). Through the gate you now have a
wall on your left; in 150y, opposite the track to East
Witton Lodge on the right, turn left and right through
a gate, so that the wall and hedge are now on the right.
There is an old-fashioned plough abandoned by the
hedge.

Still keeping your wits about you, go through a gate
and at the end of a small plantation cross a waymarked
stile. Hug the plantation as far as another waymarked
gate, then take a right and left into a hedged lane. In
200y, where the lane turns sharp right, go ahead over a
waymarked stile into a field and after 70y cross another
stile. Note its grooved stone base – probably an old
drainage stone. Follow the waymark and there are
lynchets in the next field; over another stone stile in
150y reveals a good track through the next field; and
finally into Braithwaite Lane and left to the edge of
East Witton village, and deserved refreshment.

Upper Wharfedale

The upper valley of the River Wharfe is the setting for a walk that contours along terraced hillside through limestone pastures above scar woodland. The route descends through Yockenthwaite and Hubberholme with its beautiful church.

The glacial valley of Upper Wharfedale sits in the high country at the centre of the Yorkshire Dales National Park. The start of this 7m walk is at 750f and the path climbs to heights of 1,200f before descending to the riverside at Yockenthwaite and following the Wharfe's course down to Hubberholme. There are many stiles along the way, some requiring care and agility.

Leave the car park through a gate at its northern end and take the prominent track that ascends towards and through Rakes Wood, a scrubby woodland of birch, ash, hazel and hawthorn. The trail is stony and at the top, where it emerges from the wood, it crosses bare limestone; the outer side is embanked to maintain a level surface. This track is part of the Roman road linking the fort at Bainbridge, in Wensleydale, with

▽ *The track contouring along Buckden Rake hillside*

YOCKENTHWAITE

R. Wharfe

Car park: Buckden (National Park) 20m N of Skipton, via B6265 from Skipton then B6160 from Grassington.
Grid ref: SD 934 775.

△ *Water races down from the higher fells along Cray Gill, on its way to join the River Wharfe near Buckden*

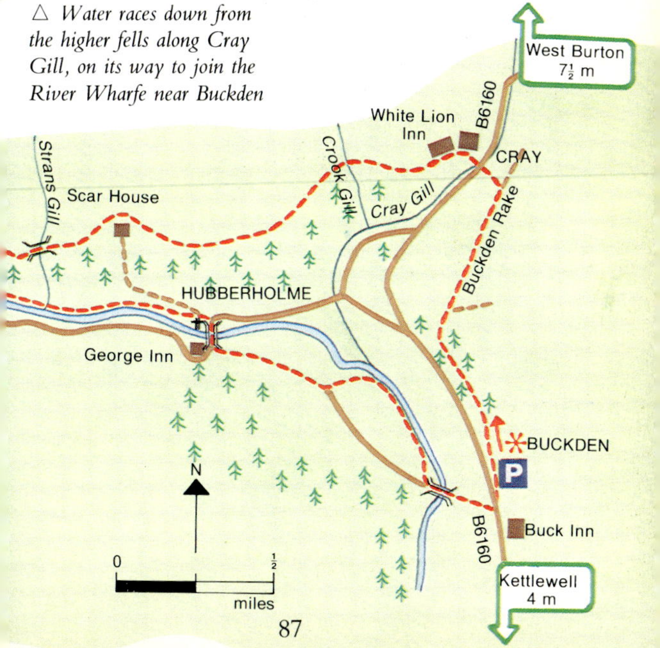

West Burton
7½ m

B6160

White Lion
Inn

CRAY

Crook Gill

Cray Gill

Buckden Rake

Strans Gill

Scar House

HUBBERHOLME

George Inn

BUCKDEN

P

Buck Inn

B6160

Kettlewell
4 m

N

0   ½
miles

87

△ *Dales sheep pass by in the shelter of a drystone wall*
▷ *Solid stonework shields the watercourse at Cray*
▷ ▽ *An idyllic scene at the hamlet of Cray, as water tumbles over rock outcrops to feed the Wharfe in the valley below*

the larger fort at Ilkley. Its course is well-defined between Bainbridge and Buckden, but only conjectured in Wharfedale.

The track levels out and swings slightly right to contour the hillside along Buckden Rake, through gates and over stiles. In ½m turn left through a small gate in the limestone wall and descend steeply to the hamlet of Cray. As you reach the road across the beck note the circular potholes in its rocky bed. These are caused by the water swirling small, hard boulders and pebbles that gradually erode the softer limestone. Pass behind the White Lion Inn (unless you are thirsty) and go through the right-hand of two gates, where the path rises diagonally across bare stone for 30y to another gate. Here a yellow waymark indicates the route, which passes some wooden hen-houses on the right. The well-built hay-barns behind the White Lion show in their walls the characteristic 'throughs', large stones projecting from the wall face that tie the outer and inner wall surfaces together.

The path is now through meadows, where you should keep in single file to avoid unnecessary trampling of valuable meadow grass. Follow the yellow waymarks through a series of gates and the path

gradually bears right to the head of Crook Gill (stream). Cross by the wooden footbridge among the rowan trees. If the stream is dry you may notice 'alien' rocks among the limestone of its bed; these are sandstones and shales of the Yoredale strata carried down from the high fell.

Beyond the footbridge turn left along the terrace. The low wall on your left exhibits small squared holes here and there – these are cripple, or sheep, holes that allow sheep but not cattle to pass through into an adjoining pasture. The wall eventually becomes a single-strand fence by an area of natural limestone 'pavement', where a few hawthorns and a lone ash tree grow. The vertical fissures in the pavement are called

grykes; the limestone slabs between are clints. Rain-water bearing minute amounts of acidic carbon dioxide erodes the weaker bands of limestone to form the grykes, while horizontal seepage below undercuts the clints. The grykes are a good home for shade-loving plants such as ferns.

Pause to take in the Wharfedale landscape. A typical glaciated valley – U-shaped, with flat floor and steep sides – the hills show long limestone scars and plenty of deciduous woodland. Most of the vegetation is the result of human interference. Langstrothdale to the right was a hunting forest for the Norman aristocracy, and Buckden was established as a forest-edge settlement for the hunting officials. Boundary walls of the

△ *The wooden footbridge over Crook Gill, on the northern section of the walk from Cray to Yockenthwaite. The soft limestone of its bed is scattered with hard sandstones carried from higher ground; these swirl in the current to erode odd-shaped holes in the limestone*
◁ *Erosion in action, as the fast-running waters cut into the layered limestone of the Wharfedale valley side*

◁ *Redstarts breed in open countryside where drystone walls make sheltered nest sites. Most depart in September for Africa*
▷ *The great tit, familiar from gardens, often flocks with other tit species outside the breeding season, when food is scarce. At other times it chases away its smaller relations to secure the lion's share of food*
▽ *The River Wharfe at Yockenthwaite*

valley fields date from the Enclosures period in the late eighteenth century, and the long straight walls up the hillsides represent the nineteenth-century allotment enclosures.

Back on the track, you skirt Hubberholme Wood and descend slightly behind Scar House to a signpost indicating *Cray, Yockenthwaite and Hubberholme*. Continue at the same level along the path for Yockenthwaite, passing through a gate with a yellow waymark by it. In 400y go through a small plantation, mainly of sycamores, and on its far side cross the spectacular little ravine of Strans Gill by a tiny stone packhorse bridge. Descend to your left to the bottom corner of the field and the path levels out, through many small fields with waymarked stiles set in limestone walls. The old walls and enclosures here,

△ *The goldcrest, one of our smallest birds, lives chiefly in coniferous woods but is also seen in other habitats*

especially those incorporating huge boulders, may be medieval in origin and represent the dwellings and enclosures of forest keepers and wardens.

The path descends again before levelling out by a wall, later replaced by a fence. Cross two stiles and a gully and walk down to the hamlet of Yockenthwaite. Past the first house there is a left turn to reach the bridge over the River Wharfe. Go through a gate and some small sheepfolds, to the field path by the riverside fence. At Yockenthwaite this path is signposted *Dales Way* and its course left to Hubberholme is indicated by waymarks, though not always distinct. The route keeps to the river's north bank and passes behind Hubberholme Church, which is well worth a visit. The long, low profile of the church, mainly fifteenth century but with an older tower, is characteristic of churches in the Dales. The rare rood-loft of 1558 is painted red, black and yellow, and most of the modern furnishings are by Thompson of Kilburn. These are of adze-finished English oak and identified by his trade-mark, a tiny mouse, usually carved in an inconspicuous place.

After the church, cross the road bridge and turn left to follow the road for about $\frac{1}{2}$m. Take the riverside path through a gate on the left, signposted *Buckden*, and arrive by another bridge across the Wharfe. Buckden is ahead, only 200y away, while the Wharfe flows on to Grassington, Ilkley, the Ouse near Selby and finally the Humber estuary.

Grange-in-Borrowdale

A long and lovely ridge walk in the high fells west of Borrowdale. The paths climb to over 2,000f at High Spy for spectacular views of the valleys on either side. The route is steep and rough in places, so this is not a walk for the inexperienced or poor weather.

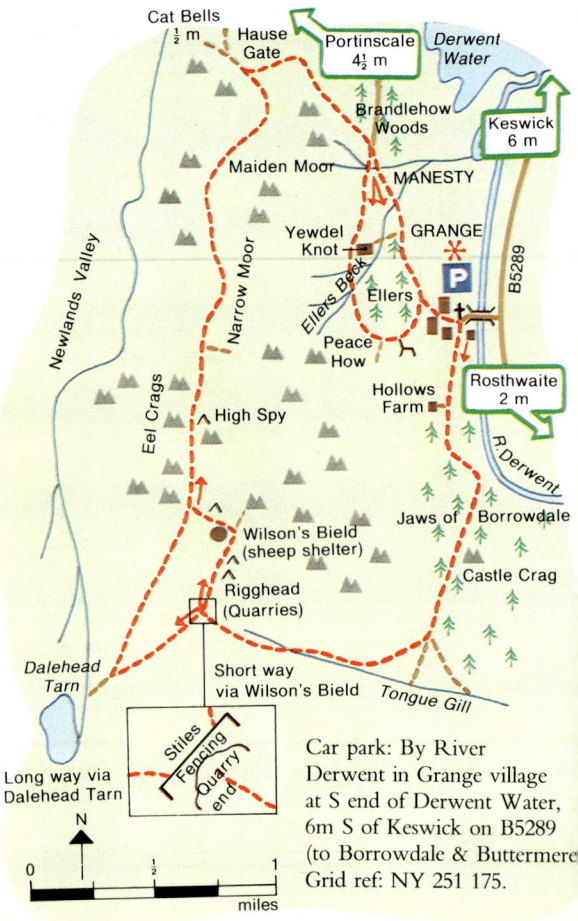

Car park: By River Derwent in Grange village at S end of Derwent Water, 6m S of Keswick on B5289 (to Borrowdale & Buttermere) Grid ref: NY 251 175.

Grange-in-Borrowdale makes an interesting start to this 7½m ridge walk, which will probably take five to six hours to complete. As you drive south from Keswick the turn-off right to Grange is over a shapely double bridge spanning the River Derwent. The hamlet of Grange, nestling among a cluster of ice-smoothed rocks, gained its name from being the chief monastic settlement in the valley, recorded as 'our grange in Borrowdale' in 1396 in the Coucher Book of Furness Abbey. Borrowdale is one of the most interesting valleys in the Lake District, both geologically and for its varied and rare plants, birds and insects. The NT own much of the lake, valley and high fells and this walk is entirely on NT land.

There is a small parking area on the west side of the bridge above the river. From the bridge walk through the village past the shop and post office and turn left just before the small church, taking the original toll road south through the valley to Honister. One of the old cottages on the left belongs to the NT and is let, as is usual policy, to a local family. Before the track reaches the river it passes a turn-off to Hollows Farm on the right. This farm marks the site where the two main rock formations of the valley, Borrowdale Volcanic series to the south-west and Skiddaw Slate to the north-east, come together and have their boundary.

To the left the Derwent runs green over its slate bed, winding in deep pools and gravel ridges through the 'Jaws of Borrowdale'. The path heads right, away from the river, and leaves the woodland through a gate to become a rough track; it is hard to imagine this was the main road up to the First World War. The track climbs and Castle Crag, the 'Tooth of Borrowdale', is on the left. Traces of an iron age fort have been found at its summit and it was given to the NT as a war memorial. The top of Castle Crag was one of the recommended viewpoints in Thomas West's *Guide to the Lakes*, published in 1778. He says of it: 'This truly secreted spot is completely surrounded by the most horrid, romantic mountains that are in this region of wonders.' The view from the cairn at the top of the col between Castle Crag and Goat Crag, looking north towards Skiddaw and the lake, is certainly very fine and the buttresses of Goat Crag opposite the 'Tooth' make an impressive rampart.

The track, now grassy, levels out along the side of the fell above Rosthwaite village, with checkered fields in the valley bottom as it widens south of the 'Jaws'. The main track dips down the fell but this walk forks to the right, away from the old road and towards a quarry track. This takes you to Rigghead Quarry, now disused. Fenced against sheep, the gates and stiles allow access to the slaty path that was probably a permanent way for rail trucks. The quarry road crosses Tongue Gill and climbs the face of the old quarry among the spoil heaps. The path is rough and steep, but the many levels and caverns give a reason to pause for a rest. Exploration, though, can be dangerous.

At the top of the quarry there is a choice of routes. A longer way is straight ahead to Dale Head Tarn, then a right turn up the main High Spy trail for those who do not like to leave a path. A shorter route takes the right-hand stile over the quarry fence to a cairned grass path and up the east face of High Spy, from where you should turn quickly left past a sheepfold – Wilson's

◁ *The River Derwent flows wide and shallow past Grange*
◁ ▽ *A view up to Grange Fell on the outward section*
▽ *Tongue Gill races down from Rigghead Quarry*

Bield – and a cairn over pathless fell. After about five minutes' walking west–north–west you join the main path up High Spy.

Turn right and head for the ridge, with breathtaking views west and north over Eel Crags into the wild country at the top of Newlands Valley. The NT has owned this area only since 1978 and a recent biological survey carried out by an NT team discovered that here, around High Scawdel and Dale Head Tarn, there are many alpine flowers including alpine meadow-rue, alpine mouse-ear and mountain sorrel. The small mountain ringlet butterfly, Britain's only alpine species, has been seen here. Raven and buzzard soar on the warm thermals and the stonechats, ring ousels and red grouse find the grasslands good feeding ground.

At last you reach the summit of High Spy (2,143f) and from the cairn, a substantial structure, there are wide views in clear weather. Looking south, the skyline is dominated by Great End, Scafell Pike, Scafell and Great Gable. To the right Dale Head, above Newlands, turns north to follow the ridge path, then the fells above Braithwaite, Bassenthwaite Lake and Skiddaw come into view.

△ *The vendace, a relative of the salmon, is an ice-age survivor that lives in Derwent Water; it also inhabits mountain lakes in Europe and around the Baltic*

◁ *The deserted slate quarries at Rigghead, memorial to the days before brick, tile and reconstituted stone. Although the piles look interesting they are unstable and should not be used for scrambling*
▽ *The cairn at the summit of High Spy marks the approximate halfway point on the walk*

△ *The small mountain ringlet butterfly has been seen around Eel Crags; its caterpillars feed on grasses*

High Spy is the start of one of the finest ridge walks in the Lake District, an almost level airy path along the top of the fells between Newlands and Borrowdale. As you head northwards the route winds between volcanic outcrops including Blea Crag, another notable viewpoint; later, on Narrow Moor above Hollows Farm, it starts a gentle descent over smooth turf that indicates the underlay of Skiddaw Slate. Narrow Moor certainly is narrow, with steep slopes to the right and precipices to the left. Walkers caught by cloud or mist should take great care to keep to the path and the cairns. Beyond Narrow Moor, with views into Newlands Valley, you cross the broader summit of Maiden Moor (1,887f). From here the path curves down, with fine views to the right over the Watendlath Fells of the Helvellyn range, to Hause Gate, the col between Maiden Moor and Cat Bells.

At Hause Gate there is a crossroads: left to Newlands, straight on for Cat Bells, and the right turn of this walk, back to Grange-in-Borrowdale. This path down the flank of the fell suffered from overuse and became a series of deep and slippery gullies, but the NT has now repaired the erosion by infilling and seeding. Stone cross-drains carry away water and the pitched stones, as once used for packhorse tracks, reinforce the most vulnerable points on the path. Manesty and

△ *Derwent Water, from high on Maiden Moor*
◁ *Grazers enjoy the fine summer pasture on Narrow Moor*

Brandelhow woods to the left clothe the lower slopes of Cat Bells with oak and beech, birch and alder. Across the valley and Derwent Water are the great ramparts of Walla Crag, more of the Borrowdale Volcanic series, and from this height it is possible to see where the River Derwent wriggles out of the reedbeds to meet its lake. Redshanks and oystercatchers have recently been reported nesting in this rush–and–mire area.

The path joins the road at the bottom of Cat Bells by Manesty Farm, where there was once a toll gate. Turn right and it is ⅔m along the road to Grange. An alternative path along the fell forks right just before you reach the road: this is about twice the distance but more than twice as interesting. After running roughly parallel with the road this path swings to the left round the grounds of Ellers, crossing Ellers Beck which is bordered by a long wall of rock. In the rock face is a cave, looking mysterious and romantic but only the result of mining activity. The path skirts a plantation and at a stile and water tank turns left on to Peace How. This area was given to the NT by Canon Rawnsley and his wife as a war memorial. Views from the seat on the hummocky ground are delightful and the path finally emerges on the road opposite the Borrowdale Gates Hotel, with the village to the right.

Safety on the Fells

Walking and scrambling in the wilder, more remote parts of our countryside can give exhilarating feelings of freedom and achievement. Unfortunately, more than 200 people each year set out on their last walk. Some of the fatalities are among experienced mountaineers or rock-climbers, well equipped but out on routes acknowledged to be dangerous. Yet many of those who die are ill-equipped, poorly prepared or often just foolhardy.

Walking is supposed to be enjoyable. One of the factors contributing to enjoyment is the knowledge and confidence that come from thorough planning, preparation, and correct equipment. None of the walks in this series is particularly arduous, but some of the longer ones may be dangerous in poor weather or for novice walkers. Certain preparations can be life-saving, so bear in mind these points.

1. Be prepared. Take waterproof anorak and overtrousers, also a spare jumper, socks, gloves and hat. Carry a whistle, small torch or some other means of attracting attention, plus energy-packed food in the form of chocolate, mint cake or glucose.

2. Detailed maps (1:25,000 or better) and compass are essential. Plan the route carefully, allowing 2 miles per hour in undulating country and 1 to $1\frac{1}{2}$ miles per hour in rocky, hilly areas. Bear in mind an 'escape route' to a main road, village or rescue post in case of bad weather or injuries.

3. Check on the weather. Combine official forecasts with 'unofficial' ones from local people with good knowledge – climbers, walkers, youth hostellers, information centre staff.

4. Allow enough time for the walk, with an hour or two to spare. Tell someone where you are going and when you expect to be back, or leave a note visible in your car.

5. The weather can close in quickly and without warning. Accept that you may have to turn back or sit tight until conditions improve; if you try to go on you may become completely lost.

6. Take a first-aid kit and know how to deal with minor injuries. Major accident victims should be kept warm and still – do not move them unless exposure is likely (see below). The emergency signal is six of something (blasts on a whistle, flashes from a torch) repeated at minute intervals.

7. Never walk alone. Go in threes, or better in fours. Don't separate. If there is an injury then one or two people go for help while the rest stay with the victim.

8. Do not drink alcohol or take drugs before you set off, and make sure everyone in the party is fit enough to undertake a long walk.

HYPOTHERMIA AND FROSTBITE

Hypothermia (exposure) is an insidious and dangerous condition in which body temperature falls from the normal 37°C to 35°C or below. It is usually caused by prolonged exposure to cold weather; it is encouraged by inadequate clothing, wet garments, high altitude, tiredness and low temperatures (the air temperature need not be below freezing point).

The signs of hypothermia are as follows: the sufferer complains of feeling cold and is cold to the touch (even on the abdomen); he or she turns pale, shivers and becomes irritable and irrational; as the condition worsens the shivering stops, speech slurs, pulse slows and the sufferer eventually loses consciousness.

When treating hypothermia, the main aim is slowly to rewarm the sufferer. Cover with warm, dry coats or blankets and move to a sheltered place. If he or she is fully conscious provide warm, sweet drinks. Send for help and arrange a medical examination at the earliest opportunity.

Frostbite only occurs in below-freezing temperatures. The affected part, usually a finger or toe, feels prickly or painful and then goes numb and cannot be moved at will. The skin is cold and hard to the touch and appears mottled or waxy-white.

To treat frostbite remove constricting clothing or similar items and gently rewarm the part.

Wansfell & Skelghyll

Wansfell, east of Ambleside and the head of
Lake Windermere, offers three walks of
varying lengths. Choose from a short ramble
through delightful woodland, a moderate and
fairly level walk across fells via Troutbeck
village, and a long walk to the heights of
Wansfell Pike.

Waterhead, at the top of Lake Windermere, is a
pleasant lakeshore hamlet and the start for each of the
three Wansfell walks. The short route of 2m takes
walkers to the splendid viewpoint of Jenkin Crag and
back through beautiful woods. The 7m moderate
walk extends this route to Troutbeck village and a visit
to Statesman's House (NT). The 8½m long walk starts
in woodland and climbs Wansfell Pike (1,597f) before
joining the moderate walk at Troutbeck.

From the steps at the back of the car park carefully
cross the main A591 road and between two guest
houses, opposite the Waterhead Hotel, is an unobtrus-
ive gap in the wall. This is reached by three steep steps
and identified by a footpath sign as the path up the
bank to Skelghyll Wood. At the top of the bank there
is a stile over the wall and the path runs diagonally
across the top pasture into the wood. The views over
Lake Windermere are worth stopping to admire.

The 190a of Skelghyll Wood have belonged to the
NT since 1957. On a high level it is largely oak; on the
lower slopes is mixed woodland with a good population of bird cherry, but also some exotic firs such as
sequoia and Hondo spruce (by far the tallest trees in the
Lake District).

The path slants uphill to the right and crosses the gill
(stream) by a substantial stone bridge built to with-
stand the demands placed on it in times of spate. Above
the gill where the track levels there is a path to the left
up to Kelsick Scar. Named after John Kelsick, the
founder of Ambleside Grammar School, this is the
highest point locally. The views are well worth the
climb unless you intend to take the long walk to

△ *Exotic firs planted on the lower slopes of Skelghyll Wood*

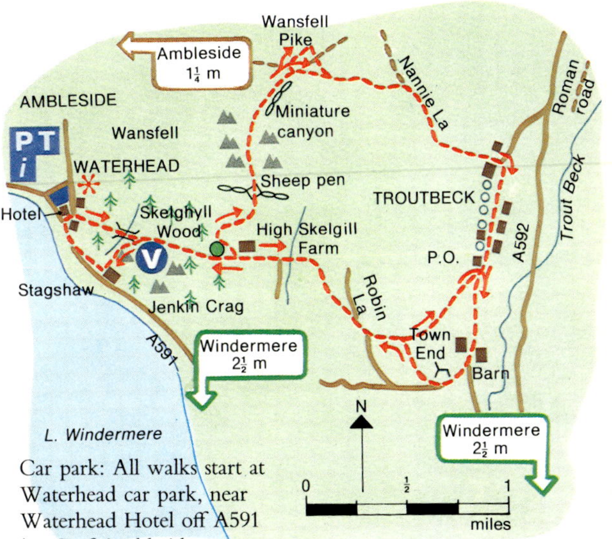

Sequoia   Hondo spruce

Ambleside
1¼ m

Wansfell
Pike

Nannie La

AMBLESIDE

Wansfell

Miniature
canyon

Roman
road

WATERHEAD

Sheep pen

TROUTBECK

Hotel

Skelghyll
Wood

High Skelgill
Farm

P.O.

A592

Trout Beck

Stagshaw

Jenkin Crag

Robin
La

Town
End

Barn

Windermere
2½ m

A591

Windermere
2½ m

N

L. Windermere

0   ½   1

miles

Car park: All walks start at
Waterhead car park, near
Waterhead Hotel off A591
½m S of Ambleside.
Grid ref: NY 378 032.

Wansfell Pike from where the views are even better.

A few yards farther the NT sign on the right heralds the viewpoint of Jenkin Crag. From the terraced rocks you can see the length of Windermere and the surrounding fells. In the oak woodlands below the rocks brown hares, red squirrels, badgers and roe deer keep well away from public paths. Many species of moths and butterflies are seen here and the 'common' toad and frog are prolific in the boggy areas.

Jenkin Crag is the turn-round point of the short walk. The return is back through the wood, but in spring it is worth turning left before the stone bridge on to a path that threads through some tall firs to Stagshaw Garden (NT). This property is open to the public only from Easter to the end of June since it is essentially a spring garden. At other times of year, or after your spring visit to Stagshaw, a fenced path to the north-west, halfway down Stagshaw Drive, makes a walk down to and along the main A591 road unnecessary. The path emerges at Waterhead, just south of the car park.

Walkers on the moderate and long routes continue from Jenkin Crag on the Troutbeck track, and it is

only a short walk to the gate at the end of the wood. Through this, wide views of Lake Windermere open out and the battlements of Wray Castle (NT) can be seen on the far shore. The track rounds the shoulder of the open fell and ahead is the gate of High Skelghyll Farm, managed by the NT both for landscape preservation and to maintain the area's traditional way of life. High Skelghyll offers welcome refreshments to the many people who take the public right of way through the farmyard to or from Troutbeck.

The moderate walk goes straight on here: through the gate, down the farm road, turn left across a bridge over the beck, then up the fellside to meet Robin Lane where a right turn takes you down into Troutbeck village. (The next section of the moderate walk is described below.)

Back at High Skelghyll Farm, the long route branches off at the sycamore tree a few yards before the gate. Turn left round the tree, almost taking a hairpin, and follow the cart-track up the fell. After the initial lift it inclines to the right and makes for the intake wall, through which there is a gate with a sheep-fold on the other side. Past the sheep-fold the path climbs through

△ *The path up to the hump of Wansfell, on the long walk*
◁ *The head of Windermere, from the slope above Waterhead*

a miniature rocky canyon, with a cairn to confirm the route, and comes out on the humped, uneven shoulder of Wansfell. Unfold the map to interpret the extensive view of the Langdales, the Fairfield horseshoe and the central fells. The path, going up the ridge on the right, is sometimes difficult to distinguish from a sheep track but there are numerous cairns dotted around to guide your way up to Wansfell Pike. Springy turf is beneath the feet, harebells grow along the walls and below is Ambleside and, later, the Kirkstone Pass.

Below Wansfell Pike still, the path from Ambleside crosses your track. This ignores the Pike itself and goes over a wall ladder that poses problems for the less agile walker and defeats most large dogs. You can turn right here or walk to the top of the Pike where another path goes north-east, then south-east off the 'nose' down to meet the trail from Ambleside.

As you wind eastwards down through the morrains there is a glimpse of the High Street precipice ahead.

◁ *Part of the extensive views from Wansfell. Looking south and west over Windermere, the town of Ambleside is tucked behind the near ridge to the right. The NT protects over 300a of high fell west of Wansfell Pike, acquired in 1982 and encompassing a Site of Special Scientific Interest*
▷ *On the long haul down from Wansfell into Trout Beck valley and Troutbeck village*

You are in a mosaic of rocky knolls, silvery with bogs where buttercups and forget-me-nots make their own mosaic. A buzzard mews over the Pike and larks sing above the grass tussocks where they nest. The path eventually comes out into Nannie Lane, an old fell road where you turn right and descend south-east on an abrupt and stony dive into Troutbeck.

Nannie Lane comes off the fell on to the Kirkstone Pass road opposite the Mortal Man inn. The sign was painted by Julius Caesar Ibbetson, a landscape artist who lived in Troutbeck from 1801 to 1805. It represents two mortal men, one rosy and fat, the other thin and miserable, with this verse painted beneath: 'Oh, mortal man, that liv'st on bread, How comes thy nose to be so red? Thou silly ass, that looks so pale, It is by drinking Birkett's Ale!'

Turn right to reach the centre of the mile-long Troutbeck village. Five wells, all dedicated to saints, are signs of a naturally prolific water supply. Beyond the post office is Robin Lane, signed to the right as a bridlepath to Skelghyll and Jenkin Crag; this is where the moderate route arrives in the village.

History goes back a long way in Troutbeck. A Roman road can be traced coming down the steep flank of Froswick from the precipice-hedged summit of High Street; the head of the valley was once a medieval deer park of 2,000a. Nearer our own time there are over a score of seventeenth- and eighteenth-century buildings in the village, a tribute to the heyday

of the Statesman farmer who grazed his flocks on the upland fells. Beatrix Potter bought the largest farm in the valley, Troutbeck Park Farm, and gave it to the NT as part of her bequest. Also NT-owned is Townend, $\frac{1}{4}$m south of the village on the road. This, the most perfectly preserved Statesman's farmhouse in the valley, belonged to the Browne family for over 400 years. The seventeenth-century farmhouse, which gives the visitor a unique glimpse into the Dalesman's way of life, has restricted opening so check ahead.

Those on moderate and long walks may return by either of two routes. First is back to Troutbeck and the bridlepath left to Skelghyll, although those following the moderate walk will have already experienced this. The second route continues on the road, south beyond Townend, and forks right on the Ambleside road. A lane to the right, where a memorial bench offers rest after the climb, joins up with Robin Lane at its far end. Take this right turn and $\frac{1}{2}$m along the lane a gate to the left, signed *Ambleside, Skelghyll and Jenkin Crag*, leads down the fell to the High Skelghyll Farm road and the familiar route back through the farm and Skelghyll Wood. A further choice is offered just before the stone bridge, as described above – either left to Stagshaw Garden or straight ahead for the more direct return to Waterhead.

◁ *The terrain around Wansfell is a patchwork of turf and boggy depressions*
△ *An open gate (on the way down from Wansfell) means someone has ignored the country code – make sure it is closed!*
▷ *Sheep at High Skelghyll Farm, managed by the NT*
▽ *Fungi, in this case fly agarics, flourish in the damp shade of Holbeck Ghyll*

Loughrigg Fell

This walk west and north from Ambleside gives beautiful views of three lakes, with a glimpse of a fourth. The terrain is ever-changing and there is a rich variety of wildflowers. A few steep sections make the route suitable only for those who are fully prepared.

Loughrigg Fell and the wild country between the lakes of Grasmere, Rydal and Windermere provide the setting for this 8½m walk. The going is generally easy and seldom rises to 1,000f but there are occasional rough patches and one steep descent to Loughrigg Terrace. As with other walks, bracken can spring up in a few days and make the paths difficult to follow.

Ambleside, at the head of Lake Windermere, is the tourist centre for southern lakeland and the beginning of the walk. There was an urban settlement in the

PATH TO
AMBLESIDE

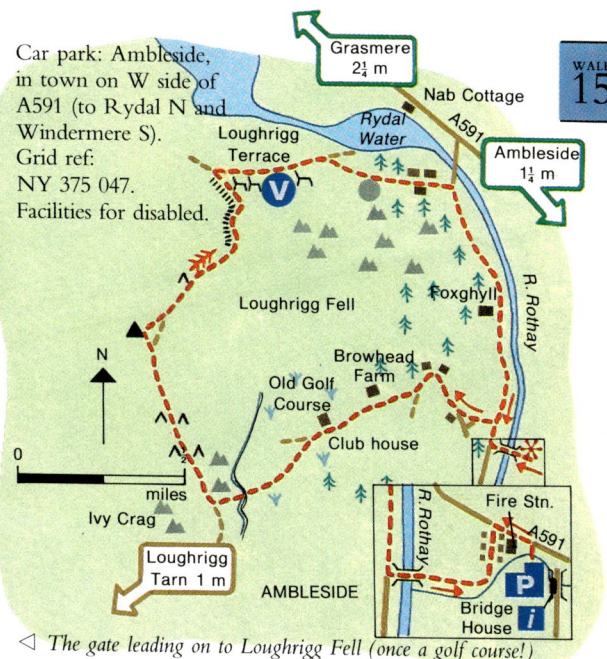

Car park: Ambleside, in town on W side of A591 (to Rydal N and Windermere S). Grid ref: NY 375 047. Facilities for disabled.

Grasmere 2¼ m

Nab Cottage

A591

Rydal Water

Ambleside 1¼ m

Loughrigg Terrace

V

Loughrigg Fell

Foxghyll

R. Rothay

N

Browhead Farm

Old Golf Course

0

Club house

miles

Ivy Crag

R. Rothay

Fire Stn.

A591

P

Bridge House

i

Loughrigg Tarn 1 m

AMBLESIDE

◁ *The gate leading on to Loughrigg Fell (once a golf course!)*

Ambleside area when the Romans manned Galava fort among the Windermere marshes. In later years it was a centre of the woollen trade with a market granted in 1650. Now it is mainly Victorian with a parish church built in 1850 by Sir Gilbert Scott. The public car park is just through the town on the left of the Rydal Road. As you leave the car park, turn right to visit one of the most unusual buildings in the town, the Old Bridge House. This is curiously placed on the crown of the bridge over Rattle Beck with one small room and a tiny room over it. It is now the NT Information Centre. Retrace your steps past the car park and turn left down Stoney Lane, a cul-de-sac of pleasant modern houses with, at the end, a signed path following the Rattle Beck across the valley. A stone-slab fence lines the path and vast ice-smoothed boulders – *rouches moutonnes* – are strewn here and there across the valley floor. A packhorse bridge spans the River Rothay to join the Under Loughrigg road where parkland trees provide shade. Turn right over a cattle grid and then directly left uphill on a public

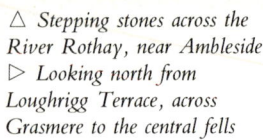

△ *Stepping stones across the River Rothay, near Ambleside*
▷ *Looking north from Loughrigg Terrace, across Grasmere to the central fells*

footpath and bridleway to Loughrigg. Before long, glance over your shoulder for opening views of the Rothay valley, Scandale Fells and Wansfell.

The path is moderately steep, and loses its tarmac surface at Browhead Farm. Near the top of the rise there is a gate, giving an opportunity to pause and look back again to see the Fairfield range. The path goes out on to fell land, though it was once an ambitious golf course. Foxgloves stand like sentinels along the wall, cottongrass waves tiny flags of truce in the dips, and juniper grows on the dryer slopes. Round the next corner is a residence called Pine Rigg, which used to be the golfers' clubhouse – the 'tenth hole'.

Past Pine Rigg there is another wall ahead, with a gate that emerges on to the Loughrigg plateau. Turn right along the wall for a short distance, then left to climb a small rise and descend into a hollow. Loughrigg is full of lumps and hollows, forming what is called 'mammilated topography', tamer in appear-

ance than the spectacular crags of the central fells. At an altitude of 1,000f the area is a mosaic of acidic grassland, bracken, rock outcrop and mire. The mires, which include small open-water pools, are rich in wetland plants such as intermediate bladderwort, oblong-leaved sundew, grass of parnassus and spike-rush. Bracken flourishes on this upland and in high summer can obscure the less obvious paths. It is as well to note the landmarks or take a compass bearing; people who fail to do this can wander in circles for hours.

The route follows the main track into the hollow and leaves it to fork right past a peat hag, with the loom of Ivy Crag to the left. The well-defined path takes a scramble over a rocky knoll and climbs the ridge to the left. There is a view of Windermere to the west and the Coniston Fells are straight ahead. The path continues along the ridge for a time, with the Langdale Pikes to the north-west, then on the next crag there is a large cairn that signals a view of Loughrigg Tarn and

Elterwater beyond, with the long gleam of Coniston Water to the left. The small valley in front, almost a miniature glen, has several large cairns to keep the traveller on the right road. At the head of the glen the path turns left and uphill to the highest point on Loughrigg, 1,001f, where there is a survey grid. Grasmere Fells and the crags of Silver How can be seen away to the north-west, at the far end of Grasmere Lake. The track along the ridge is thought to have been a prehistoric route used by neolithic men for the transport of axeheads. These were chipped out in the 'axe factories' on the Langdale Pikes and found their way all over England. The route would have been south-west over the summits of Silver How and Loughrigg Fell, down to Ambleside and the lake.

The path goes on over the nose of the crag and down the slope towards Grasmere, passing a large cairn from which the vale of Grasmere and the surrounding fells are a pleasure to the eye. After the cairn there is a steep, rough section and although the River Rothay and Rydal Water are beautiful it is better to watch the path and leave the view to itself. Much erosion repair work has been done on this slope, with scars filled in and rock steps built on the last section to prevent further crumbling of the fellside.

Almost literally you drop on to Loughrigg Terrace, and everything is suddenly calm and beautiful. This is one of the best-loved paths in the Lake District and the route is right, towards Rydal. From the Terrace there is a perfect prospect of Grasmere, so full of associations with William Wordsworth. When he made Dove Cottage his home he wrote, 'Can the choice mislead, That made the calmest, fairest spot on earth, With all its unappropriated good, My own.'

Beyond Grasmere Lake the road climbs over Dunmail Raise – they used to say in Westmorland that 'now't good comes over't Raise ferm Cummerland'. To the left of the Raise is Helm Crag, topped by the strange rock shaped like a lion and a lamb. The terraced track dips gently towards the river and makes for a wall, but before you reach it a path forks to the right and goes along the fellside. Before taking it, it is worth looking back at the view with the nob of Pike O'Stickle, site of one of the axe factories, peering over the Grasmere Fells left of centre. Rydal Water, below

Grass of parnassus

Bladderwort

Plants of acid, boggy areas thrive on the Loughrigg plateau. Bladderwort and sundew compensate for the mineral deficiencies by trapping and digesting small insects; grass of parnassus also has glands that attract insects

Sundew

the level fellside track, is ruffled by the breeze and across the water Nab Cottage gleams white under the impressive buttress of Nab Scar.

Carry on over a rise and there is a surprise drop on to a man-made plateau of blue slate-spoil. To the right is Rydal Cave, also man-made by quarrying out the fellside for slate. The cavern is said to be large enough to accommodate the whole population of Ambleside – in the unlikely event of them all wishing to enter it. Take the quarry road down through a fine stand of Scots pine, past the lower cave and into the valley. The path descends by way of an oak wood beside a stream. A gate, then a lane, lead to the Under Loughrigg road at Pelter Bridge where you turn right to stroll beside the Rothay. Two men of note liked the spot and lived here. One was de Quincey, who lived for a time at Fox Ghyll (½m from Pelter Bridge on the right) and whose ghost is reputed to haunt one of the rooms. More usefully, de Quincey is said to have invented backpacking. He was the first to carry a tent, self-built, on his walks because he found lodging houses too expensive. Dr Arnold of Rugby School went so far as to build his own house, just beyond Fox Ghyll, and called it Fox How. As you pass it there is another mile of road before the walk comes full circle, to the packhorse bridge over the Rothay and the path through the valley to Ambleside town.

Malham Tarn

Malham is the centre for the superb walking country of craggy scenery and limestone rock features in the south Dales. Walkers should be prepared for awkward rock scrambles up Gordale Scar and into Dry Valley, but the rewards are beautiful views and the fascinating rock formations characteristic of limestone uplands.

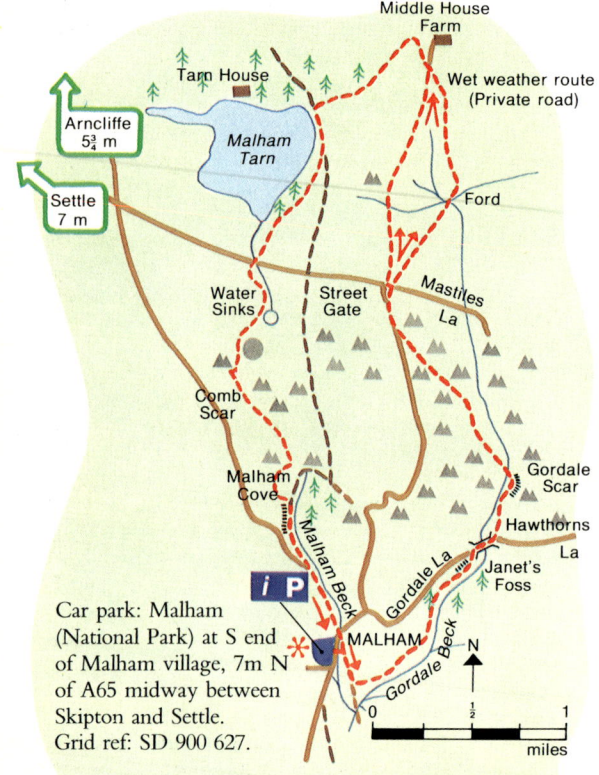

Middle House Farm

Tarn House

Wet weather route (Private road)

Arncliffe 5¾ m

Malham Tarn

Settle 7 m

Ford

Water Sinks

Street Gate

Mastiles La

Comb Scar

Gordale Scar

Malham Cove

Hawthorns La

Malham Beck

Gordale La

Janet's Foss

i **P**

MALHAM

Gordale Beck

N

Car park: Malham (National Park) at S end of Malham village, 7m N of A65 midway between Skipton and Settle. Grid ref: SD 900 627.

0   ½   1

miles

The first section of this long but absorbing 9m ramble, from Malham to Gordale Lane, has already been described in walk 9. The route is then over Gordale Scar and north to the lovely Malham Tarn lake, returning to the village past the crags, scars, pots and sinks typical of limestone scenery.

For the first section of the route, from Malham village to the waterfall at Janet's Foss, turn to walk 9. Past the fall the path emerges from the woodland by a short rock-cut staircase where you turn right into Gordale Lane. In about 250y follow the signpost left to *Gordale Scar* whose precipitous limestone cliffs dominate the immediate view to the north. Follow the path towards the narrowing gorge, and at its approach keep to the base of the cliffs on the right. The way up the gorge is by clambering up the central screen of tufa using the holds and hollows for feet and hands. Wooden steps concentrate the exit from the climb, and reduce further erosion to the path.

Before the last ice age Gordale Scar was a huge cavern, but the roof subsequently collapsed. Its tufa

△ *The narrowing, rocky track to Gordale Scar makes an imposing scramble on the outward section of the walk*

screen is often covered with waterfalls, and the hole in the rock through which the top fall cascades is probably part of the original cave.

At the top of the Scar the gradient eases and the stony track slants to the left of Gordale Valley, out on to a sheep-cropped level limestone plateau. Signposts direct you towards Malham Tarn, but well before seeing the water the path crosses a stile in a wall and puts you on to a road. Ignore the temptations of the road and keep to the track which closely follows the wall on your right. At Street Gate (NT sign) go through the gate and cut diagonally north-west across the field, rising slightly. Eventually an intersection of many walls reveals itself $\frac{1}{4}$m ahead. Aim for this, go through the gate, negotiate the ford, and head due north, aiming for Middle House Farm just over $\frac{1}{2}$m away. As you near the farm its approach track is easily identified by a ladder stile and a gate. Beyond and opposite is another ladder stile, signposted *Malham Tarn*, that points the way. The grassy track heads south-west, at the outward limit of the walk.

△ *Malham Cove looms in the distance, a splendid semi-circle of overhanging limestone with the infant River Aire rising below it*

△ *The red squirrel is to be seen in quieter moments in the area. Its summer coat is the distinctive russet-red, but in winter this turns greyish; however, the ear tufts become prominent in the colder months, allowing this species to be distinguished from the grey squirrel, which has no ear tufts*
◁ *The path on an easier, higher section of Gordale Scar*

In ¾m drop down to the prominent track (*Pennine Way* and *Nature Trail*) running south and west along the eastern edge of Malham Tarn. This natural lake rests on impervious Silurian slate brought near the surface by the North Craven Fault. Tarn House, on the north shore, is part of the NT Malham Tarn property and is leased to the Field Studies Council. Charles Kingsley used the setting for part of *The Water Babies*, and the Tarn and its shores are a designated Nature Reserve and Bird Sanctuary.

Continue on the trail to the gate, leave the Pennine Way track and bear slightly right to aim for the left-hand corner of the wood ahead. Continue this alignment until you join the Malham Moor road by a

△ Not only humans walk the Pennine Way! These sheep have taken to the long-distance footpath near Malham Tarn. The Way skirts the western and northern shores of Malham Tarn on its 250m route from Edale in the Peak District, via the Dales and the Northumberland National Park to Kirk Yetholm, just over the border near Kelso. However, it is unlikely these woolly walkers will cover the full distance

◁ Gazing down from the limestone cliff of Malham Cove, neat Dales walls criss-cross the pasture and rough grazing land

cattle grid at Water Sinks Gate. Cross the grid, cross the road and Malham Water, and go south through the new gate opposite. Soon bear left slightly to aim for the depression of Water Sinks. This is one of a number of potholes, obscured by gravel and stones, where Malham Water vanishes underground – to reappear at Airehead Springs, $\frac{1}{4}$m below Malham village. You can identify the former line of the stream as a grassy valley eventually leading to a rocky gorge.

Ignore the ladder stile opposite Water Sinks and continue down the grassy valley as it becomes narrow and stony. It leads to an impressive limestone gorge between the high cliffs of Comb Scar, with a cave on the east side. The path emerges at the top of a 'dry waterfall' almost 80f above the side of another valley, named the Watlowes but commonly known as Dry Valley. This was formed during the later stages of the last ice age, when meltwaters from Malham Tarn and the snowfields around surged down the valley; because the cracks in the limestone were ice-sealed, the water

△ Fissured limestone pavement below Comb Scar and above Malham Cove, the work of centuries of rain, ice and sun
▷ Great Close Scar, another fine limestone feature

flowed above ground to create Dry Valley. As the climate became milder the fissures unfroze and the surface waters again disappeared underground.

Follow the path as it descends to the left, and work your way down Dry Valley. To describe it as walking makes it sound too simple: it is a rough and rocky scramble. In about $\frac{1}{2}$m this valley opens out on to the top pavement of Malham Cove. The Cove is a curved cliff of limestone almost 300f high and 1,000f broad, an ancient waterfall formed by a stream flowing over the scarp of the North Craven Fault. Pause as you regain your breath to admire the superb limestone scenery.

Walk to the west end of the Cove, taking care as you cross the clints — blocks of limestone both fissured vertically and undercut by erosion — since they are smooth, and some are unstable. Cross a ladder stile and descend by the Pennine Way track, stepped in wood for safety, to the foot of the Cove. The way back to Malham is now straight ahead, joining the road that runs south through the village to the start.

Useful information

The NT owns and protects well over 500,000a in England, Wales and Northern Ireland – about one per cent of the total land area. It is perhaps best known for its great country houses with their gardens and parks, but it was not for these that the organization came into existence in 1895. At that time the countryside itself and its smaller buildings were under threat, as towns and suburbs spread and places like the Lake District began to feel the full impact of the newly-mobile population. The first property acquired by the NT was a mere 4½a of clifftop at Dinas Oleu, near Barmouth in Gwynedd. Its first building was the historic but modest mid fourteenth-century Clergy House at Alfriston, East Sussex.

Today, the NT looks after 450m of the finest unspoilt coastline. It has 1,100 tenanted farms, and cares for one-quarter of the Lake District National Park and one-tenth of Snowdonia. There are huge tracts of NT land in the Peak District, South Wales, Dorset and Somerset, together with parts of the Malvern and Shropshire Hills and the Isle of Wight, and there are innumerable other NT properties scattered across the country.

When you are walking on NT land, look searchingly at your surroundings. Note how the woods, fields and copses are managed, how the paths are laid out and maintained, and how local features such as stiles, walls, barns and fences are looked after and renovated in keeping with the character of the countryside.

The NT's twin aims of access and conservation take time and money. The work is based on detailed management plans, often drawn up in consultation with bodies such as the Nature Conservancy Council, Countryside Commission, local county councils, and naturalists' and archaeological trusts. Walkers who gain pleasure from NT facilities can reciprocate by joining the NT – a charity that looks after large tracts of land and buildings for you, and for future generations, to enjoy for ever.

The National Trust, Central Office, 36 Queen Anne's Gate, London SW1H 9AS; phone 01-222 9251

Membership enquiries to: The National Trust, Membership Department, PO Box 30, Beckenham, Kent BR3 4TL; phone 01-650 7263

The National Trust, **North West Regional Office** (for the Lake District), Rothay Holme, Rothay Road, Ambleside, Cumbria LA22 OEJ; phone Ambleside (09663) 3883

The National Trust, **Yorkshire Regional Office**, Goddards, 27 Tadcaster Road, York YO2 2QG; phone York (0904) 702021

Lake District National Park Information Service, Bank House, High Street, Windermere, Cumbria

Yorkshire Dales National Park Information Centre, Colvend, Hebden Road, Grassington, near Skipton, North Yorkshire BD23 5LB

Cumbria Trust for Nature Conservation, Church Street, Ambleside, Cumbria LA22 OBU

Lancashire Naturalists' Trust, Cuerden, Valley Park, Cuerden Pavilion, Bamber Bridge, Preston PR5 6AX

Yorkshire Wildlife Trust, 20 Castlegate, York YO1 1RP

Ramblers' Association, 1/5 Wandsworth Road, London SW8 2LJ; phone 01-582 6878

Ordnance Survey, Romsey Road, Maybush, Southampton SO9 4DH

Walkers are advised to plan their outings using current NT information for details of opening days and times and admission fees. Two invaluable sources are *Properties of the National Trust* and the *Properties Open* booklets relating to the region in question.

Acknowledgements

Thanks are due to Elizabeth Battrick and Geoffrey Wright for devising routes and writing walk accounts and features.

Thanks also to the following for their help:
Nigel Sale, Tiffany Hunt, Ramblers' Association

Illustrations by Andrew Aloof, Rosalind Hewitt, Elsa Willson, Michael McGuinness

Walk and locator map   Cooper West

Art work visualiser   Mike Trier

The publishers are grateful to the following companies and individuals:
Blacks of Holborn for camping equipment, Nikon UK Ltd for camera equipment, Fred and Kathy Gill, Format Publishing Service, Diana Greenman and Jane Parker